1990

MALPRACTICE AND LIABILITY IN CLINICAL OBSTETRICAL NURSING

Aspen Series in Obstetrical and Gynecological Nursing

Diane J. Angelini, MN, CNM, CNA, Series Editor
Assistant Director of Perinatal Nursing
Brigham and Women's Hospital
Boston, Massachusetts

Electronic Fetal Monitoring

Cydney I. Afriat, CNM, MSN

MALPRACTICE AND LIABILITY IN CLINICAL OBSTETRICAL NURSING

Sarah D. Cohn, RN, MSN, JD
Associate Counsel
Yale New Haven Hospital
New Haven, Connecticut

Aspen Series in Obstetrical and Gynecological Nursing
Diane J. Angelini, MN, CNM, CNA, Series Editor

AN ASPEN PUBLICATION®
Aspen Publishers, Inc.
Rockville, Maryland
1990

Library of Congress Cataloging-in-Publication Data

Cohn, Sarah D.
Malpractice and liability in clinical obstetrical nursing / Sarah D. Cohn
p. cm.
Includes bibliographical references.
ISBN: 0-8342-0141-0
1. Nurses—Malpractice—United States. 2. Obstetrical nursing—Law and legislation—United States. I. Title.
[DNLM: 1. Legislation, Nursing—United States. 2. Malpractice—United States—legislation. 3. Obstetrical Nursing—United States—legislation. WY 44 C678m]
KF2915.N83C64   1990
346.7303'32—dc20
[347.306332]
DNLM/DLC
for Library of Congress
89-18588
CIP

Editorial Services: Lorna Perkins

Library of Congress Catalog Card Number: 89-18588
ISBN: 0-8342-0141-0

Printed in the United States of America

1 2 3 4 5

Table of Contents

Preface

Malpractice and Liability in Clinical Obstetrical Nursing began in 1986 as the result of a telephone call from an editor at Aspen Publishers, Inc., to discuss the idea of a book on risk management in obstetrics. Three questions were immediately apparent: (1) how to define the scope of "risk management" (currently a very popular concept), (2) how to delineate the breadth of "obstetrics," and (3) how to consider the many health care providers who interface with obstetrical patients in hospitals and in office/clinic settings. Clearly, the book could not be written until these difficult questions were answered. My training and experience provided the background in which I found the answers.

My professional training is in nursing, nurse-midwifery, and law. I was a practicing nurse-midwife for seven years before going to law school and have maintained an active association with the American College of Nurse-Midwives and with other groups of nurses practicing in my area. These relationships have kept me up to date with many of the current concerns in clinical obstetrical practice.

I have been an associate counsel in the Risk Management/Medicolegal Affairs office at Yale School of Medicine and Yale New Haven Hospital since graduating from law school in early 1983. Yale New Haven Hospital has nearly 6,000 births per year and includes an active community- and university-based obstetrical and gynecological practice. My work at Yale and in the surrounding communities has provided me with ongoing clinical experience in health law and has contributed greatly to the practical focus of this book. I am particularly grateful to the groups of nurses with whom I have spoken over the years. As they sought answers to their questions, they gave me valuable experience in the variations of practice and practice settings and knowledge about the depth of their concerns for patient care.

Obstetrics needs to be defined broadly in order to include a number of classic gynecological topics. No book on risk management in obstetrics can omit liability concerns involving in vitro fertilization technologies, prenatal diagnosis, abortion, and sterilization. Risk management should reduce risks to individual health care providers and to the corporate institution (hospital) as problems are noted. Hopefully, this occurs before patients are injured. This book addresses liability issues in both hospital and outpatient settings.

Various skilled health care personnel practice obstetrics: nurses, nurse-midwives, obstetric/gynecologic nurse practitioners and clinical specialists, physician assistants, and physicians. Key themes of this book are collaboration and cooperation among professionals who care for patients. Risk management concepts are especially important where the members of nursing and medical staffs are not communicating or where there is conflict. These concepts are much easier to implement and are much more successful when the staff function is collaborative.

With cooperative practice in mind, I have not attempted to elaborate on every possible nursing function in each chapter. Instead, I have indicated what tasks are needed and how they should be done. For example, where ultrasound is done for prenatal diagnosis, a properly trained nurse may be the sonographer, the genetics counselor, the office manager, the primary patient contact, or some combination of these. While the outlines of obstetric nursing are varied and pervasive, risk management concerns are common to all health care personnel.

I have tried, above all, to keep this book practical. Case law has been chosen to illustrate where possible. Health law is not just theory. Actual events and cases are often the best teachers, even though the facts of each event can be complicated and involve more than one type of health care provider. Where the most illustrative case involves a physician, but the point is relevant to nursing practice, I have used it. By doing this and by citing liberally from the medical and legal literature, as well as from the nursing literature, I have tried to emphasize my view that collaborative practice is both practical and a good risk management technique. This book is for the practitioner.

As I complete this book, I gratefully recall people who have offered assistance and fondly remember events intertwined with the writing process. Portions of the manuscript have been read by several people both within and outside of the health professions. Their constructive criticisms have helped me to make the topics inclusive and readable.

Among those who have read all or part of the manuscript are Mardee and Robert Gramen, Nancy Kraus, Angela Holder, Virginia Roddy, and my husband Frederick. My young sons, although too young to read the manuscript, were interested in the writing process and particularly in the computer. Soon enough they learned not to touch the screen before I saved the file. I smiled as they helped me feed the paper into the printer.

Chapter 1

Risk Prevention and Management

1

Risk management in health care is a relatively new concept. Iatrogenic complications during health care have always occurred, but the organized study of risk to patients, visitors, and staff has begun to develop only during the past 15 years. Many professionals believe that the development of formal risk management programs within health care institutions received its impetus during the malpractice crisis of the mid-1970s.[1]

The increase in the number of professional liability cases during the mid-1970s also confirmed the demise of the legal doctrine of charitable immunity upon which many nonprofit hospitals had depended for protection. On the basis of an English decision of 1846, many American courts had held that charities were immune from tort liability.[2] Although the English soon abrogated that immunity, American courts continued to apply the doctrine. Donations to charities, it was said, would decrease if the charities were held liable, and the imposition of liability would divert trust assets from their original purposes. Further, courts held that when care was charitably rendered, the beneficiary assumed any risk of negligent treatment and that the doctrine of respondeat superior should not apply to charities. Either by case law or by statute, nearly every state has now abrogated the doctrine of charitable immunity.

Potential hospital liability was altered even further with the case of *Darling v. Charleston Community Memorial Hospital* in 1966. The facts involved an 18-year-old man who broke his leg while playing college football. He was taken to the emergency room of a local hospital where his leg was evaluated, casted, and placed in traction. Not long after the application of the cast, the patient's toes became dark and swollen, but the cast was not removed until three days later. Ultimately, the patient underwent a below-the-knee amputation of his leg because subsequent physicians were not able to repair the damage caused by the cast that was too tight. Although the defendant hospital argued that it was not liable because it did not practice medicine, that it was not liable for any nursing negligence because the nurse was simply executing the physician's order (and the order was not negligent on its face), and that once it had selected reasonable physicians, it had no further duty to assure that their care was adequate, the court found otherwise.

In affirming the lower court judgment against the hospital, the court found that the hospital had a corporate duty to review the quality of the work even of nonemployed physicians who practiced on the premises. It further found that a jury could have believed that the nursing staff did not test often enough for circulation changes caused by the cast. Once the nursing staff did detect such changes, the nurses undertook a duty to notify the attending physician. If the physician did not respond, hospital authorities were to be notified so that no irreversible harm could come to the patient.[3]

The *Darling* case has been called the most significant malpractice case of the 1960s. The opinion had immediate effects on other courts, on state agencies responsible for hospital licensing, and on hospital accreditation standards. Those effects continue to the present.

DEFINITIONS OF RISK MANAGEMENT

A risk can be defined as an exposure to possible personal injury or financial loss. Risk management first developed as loss control and reacted only after the loss had already occurred. More recently, risk management has begun to include techniques to control or prevent risks initially. Thus, risk management is now defined to include the identification, evaluation, reduction, and elimination of potential and actual risks. The definition need not be that broad but rather depends upon the application of the definition. See Exhibit 1–1 for the current definition

Exhibit 1-1 Joint Commission Definition of Risk Management

The Standards pertaining to risk management in this Manual address only those risk management functions relating to clinical and administrative activities designed to identify, evaluate, and reduce the risk of patient injury associated with care. The full scope of risk management functions encompasses activities in health care organizations that are intended to conserve financial resources from loss. These functions include a broad range of administrative activities intended to reduce losses associated with patient, employee, or visitor injuries; property loss or damages; and other sources of potential organizational liability. Many of these activities are beyond the scope of Joint Commission standards.

Source: Reprinted from *Accreditation Manual for Hospitals: 1990*, p. 311, with permission of the Joint Commission on Accreditation of Healthcare Organizations, Chicago, ©1989.

---

and its expressed limitations used by the Joint Commission on Accreditation of Healthcare Organizations (Joint Commission).

Risk management is used in all types of businesses, and in each, including health care, the techniques adopted are those relevant to the types of losses that occur in the business. Risks in health care environments are broader than health care providers would first anticipate. The business of providing health care has become complicated. Many hospitals, for example, have in-house engineering and metal shops, engage in fire prevention planning, and manage potentially toxic chemotherapeutic substances and other chemicals. Their employees must lift and move heavy and incapacitated patients, and they also face potential general and professional liability risks. While this book concentrates on patient care and some employee risks, a health care facility's concerns in its risk management section are more extensive.

SOURCES OF RISK MANAGEMENT REQUIREMENTS

The Joint Commission began to focus its attention formally on risk management in 1986. Four principles served as guidelines for the development of these first risk management standards:

1. The standards were to foster "active and appropriate" practitioner involvement in the identification of major areas of clinical risk, the

development of criteria for the identification of cases with unacceptable risk, and the design of programs to reduce clinical risk and to assist in the correction of problems identified by risk management activities.

2. The standards were to foster appropriate linkage and communication between risk management and quality assurance personnel and functions.
3. The standards were to foster the accessibility of data between quality assurance and risk management.
4. The standards were to evaluate risk by requiring the consideration of professional liability issues at the time of physician appointment and reappointment to the medical staff.[4]

The first risk management standards were adopted in 1987 and appeared in the Joint Commission's *Accreditation Manual for Hospitals: 1989*. The manual's glossary defined risk management for Joint Commission purposes as limited to those risks involving patient care. Joint Commission standards are applicable to facilities that it accredits. The standards are not explicitly applicable to other institutions and to private offices, although they are considered quite authoritative as guidelines. Further, certain states implicitly delegate some of the hospital licensing and inspection function to an accreditor by limiting the scope of evaluation by state personnel as long as the facility is accredited.

As of January 1, 1989, at least ten states had adopted either legislatively or through state regulations risk management reporting systems (see Exhibit 1–2). These systems range from very detailed reporting of patient-related incidents required in New York[5] to the Connecticut requirements (not part of a formal state-required risk management program) that a hospital report when it has taken action against a physician to limit or restrict privileges for clinical reasons.[6] When a state agency receives risk management reporting information, it may begin an investigation into the circumstances involving the hospital or the licensed health care provider.

The federal government has developed an interest in some types of risk management. For example, the Health Care Financing Administration (HCFA) has contracted with local peer review organizations to monitor hospital use and quality of care for Medicare patients.[7] Payment for

Exhibit 1–2   States with Risk Management Requirements for Hospitals

State:	Year effective:
Alaska	1976
Colorado	1988
Florida	1985
Kansas	1986
Maryland	1986
Massachusetts	1986
New York	1985
North Carolina	1987
Rhode Island	1979
Washington	1986

Source: Reprinted from *Health Care: Initiatives in Hospital Risk Management*, by United States General Accounting Office, p. 20 (GAO/HRD 89-79), July 1989.

services may be denied if the care provided is judged inappropriate or inadequate. Providers, both individual and institutional, also can be suspended from participation in the Medicare program. Congress passed the Health Care Quality Improvement Act of 1986,[8] which among other things encourages participation in good-faith peer review activities by conferring immunity from actions for damages if certain conditions are met.

Finally, professional organizations, such as the American College of Obstetricians and Gynecologists, the Nurses' Association of the American College of Obstetricians and Gynecologists, and the American College of Nurse-Midwives, have encouraged their members to learn about and participate in risk management activities, both in hospitals and in offices. To that end, many of these organizations have published educational materials designed to assist providers with general principles of these activities.

GOALS OF RISK MANAGEMENT

It has been estimated that as many as one-third of all hospitalized patients experience at least one iatrogenic incident.[9] Despite this, the number of harmed patients who actually make a claim may be less than five percent, although more patients now seem to perceive events or outcomes as negative.[10]

Risk management has three main goals. Its primary goal is to reduce the number and severity of patient, visitor, and employee injuries. Current risk management systems try to accomplish this in several ways. Hospitals, clinics, and offices have developed more formal methods of evaluating the credentials of prospective employees and medical staff and evaluating patient care rendered by health care professionals on their staffs. A formal connection between the risk management and quality assurance functions, particularly within a health care facility, should help to identify those providers whose patients experience clinical outcomes that compare unfavorably with those of similar patients.

Although it may be impossible to eliminate all injuries in a health care setting, risk management systems can collect data that may demonstrate patterns in outcomes or injuries so that corrective actions can be taken. For example, health care providers are often reminded that they must read medication labels prior to administering medication. Periodically they may neglect to do so, and medication errors then occur. Even the most intensive in-service education, however, will not prevent all errors resulting from carelessness. A medication error tracking system will demonstrate if a particular medication is more often involved in errors. When a medication is identified in this manner, the hospital or office can consider alternatives, for example, different packaging of the medication, addition of a harmless color to a liquid, or tighter controls on availability.

Finally, effective risk management, in its attempt to reduce injuries, must look at the health care facility as a whole to identify those situations having the potential for repetition and for legal action by patients or visitors. After potential problems are identified, the office or facility may consider drafting policies or procedures to guide staff members. For example, some hospitals have drafted procedures to be followed where the patient has a living will or where surgery is to be performed on a patient who is a member of Jehovah's Witnesses.

The second goal of a risk management system is to ensure that the care given a patient is adequately documented so that a possible professional liability claim can be adequately defended. Medical record committees in hospitals and periodic record reviews in offices often reveal documentation deficiencies by particular providers or categories of providers. With this information, education of the staff can be emphasized along with potential penalties for noncompliance, such as suspension of medical staff privileges for physician failure to complete medical records within the required time.

Risk management's third goal is to protect the health care provider and health care institution against financial loss by assuring the availability of adequate professional and general liability insurance.

HEALTH CARE PERSONNEL

Credentials and Qualifications

A health care facility or private practice has a legal obligation to ensure that individuals who deliver patient care on its behalf possess the credentials and skills necessary to perform their jobs competently. Although education and skills cannot prevent an occasional error or lapse in judgment, they provide at least some assurance of a provider's qualifications.

Hospitals evaluate physician credentials through the medical staff office. Medical staff bylaws, rules, and regulations set forth qualifications required for physician and nonphysician membership on the medical staff. The hospital should require an application for privileges and references from both physician and nonphysician applicants to the staff. Although a medical license is not limited to specialty practice, hospitals require that applicants for privileges apply in a particular department, such as family medicine or ophthalmology. Within each hospital department, many institutions are now requiring physicians and nurse practitioners to complete a delineation of clinical privileges. The applicant for appointment (or for renewal) must select the specialty procedures or surgeries that he or she proposes to do. The appointments process may then consider whether to approve privileges for the requested procedures.

After the hospital has received the completed application, it should verify that the applicant is licensed to practice, has obtained the degrees claimed, and has any required professional liability insurance. Although older physicians may be "grandfathered," it is now common for medical staff rules to require that a physician become board-certified in the relevant specialty within a few years of appointment to the medical staff. Failure to obtain board certification in accordance with these rules may result in the physician losing privileges to practice at that hospital.

The Joint Commission now requires that a hospital consider a physician's professional liability history during the credentialing process.[11] The Health Care Quality Improvement Act of 1986 provides some additional protection to those who participate in professional peer review actions as long as certain conditions are met.[12] A portion of the law, the implementation of which was delayed initially pending funding and is now awaiting organizational details, requires the reporting of certain information from "each entity (including an insurance company) which makes payment under a policy of insurance, self-insurance, or otherwise in settlement (or partial settlement) of, or in satisfaction of a judgment in, a medical malpractice action or claim. . . ."[13]

Recently issued federal regulations require that the information listed in Exhibit 1-3 be reported on physicians, dentists, and "other health care practitioners." For the purposes of the Health Care Quality Improvement Act and its implementing regulations, a health care practitioner is "an individual other than a physician or dentist, who is licensed or otherwise authorized by a State to provide health care services."[14]

The failure to report a payment that should have been reported can result in a $10,000 fine per omission. The law requires a state agency that revokes, suspends, or otherwise restricts a physician's license to report those facts. It further requires that a health care entity that takes a professional review action resulting in the suspension of physician clinical privileges, or the surrender of privileges while the physician is under investigation or to avoid investigation, report this information to the state board of medical examiners, which will in turn report the information to the National Practitioner Data Bank. Reporting of this type of information about other health care practitioners is voluntary, not mandatory (see Table 1-1). When this system is established, a hospital must request information from the National Practitioner Data Bank at the time any physician or other licensed health care practitioner applies for privileges and once every two years for every current member of the medical staff. The law notes that, with respect to a medical malpractice action, a

Exhibit 1–3   National Practitioner Data Bank

Information to be reported about the physician, dentist, or other health care provider:

Name

Work address

Home address (if known)

Social Security number

Date of birth

Name of each professional school attended with year of graduation

For each professional license: the number, field of licensure, and the name of the state or territory that issued it

Drug Enforcement Administration registration number (if known)

Name of each hospital with which the practitioner is affiliated (if known)

Information to be reported about the claim:

Information about the entity or person making the malpractice payment

When the claim has been filed with an adjudicative body: the name of that body and the case number

The date(s) on which the act(s) or omission(s) occurred that gave rise to the action or claim

Date of judgment or settlement

Amount paid, date of payment, and whether the payment is for a judgment or settlement, along with any conditions affecting payment

A description of the act(s) or omission(s) and injuries claimed

Classification of those acts or omissions in accordance with a system to be adopted by the Secretary

Source: Excerpted from "National Practitioner Data Bank for Adverse Information on Physicians and Other Health Care Providers," in *Federal Register* 54, pp. 42722–42734, October 1989.

Table 1-1 Reporting to the Data Bank

Entity/Action	Physicians and Dentists	Other Licensed Health Care Practitioners
Medical Malpractice Insurers A payment resulting from settlement or judgment	Must report	Must report
State Licensing Boards Adverse licensure actions	Must report	None*
Hospitals and Other Health Care Entities Adverse actions against clinical privileges	Must report	May report
Professional Societies Adverse membership actions	Must report	May report

*Must report when the requirements of Section 5 of Pub. L. 100-93 are implemented

Source: Reprinted from *Guidance for Hospitals and Other Health Care Facilities*, Regional Conference for Hospitals and Other Health Care Entities, by National Practitioner Data Bank, 1990.

hospital that does not request information about a particular applicant is presumed to have knowledge of anything the National Practitioner Data Bank contains.[15]

The federal regulations will become effective on the day that the National Practitioner Data Bank becomes operational, and that date is to be published in the *Federal Register*. Reporting of information will be prospective only, beginning with payments made or actions to be reported on or after the effective date of the regulations (see Figure 1-1).

Once information is in the Data Bank, the information will be provided upon request (and after payment of a to-be-determined fee) to a health care provider requesting information about himself or herself, to state licensing boards, to health care entities who have or are considering an employment or affiliation relationship with a health care provider or are

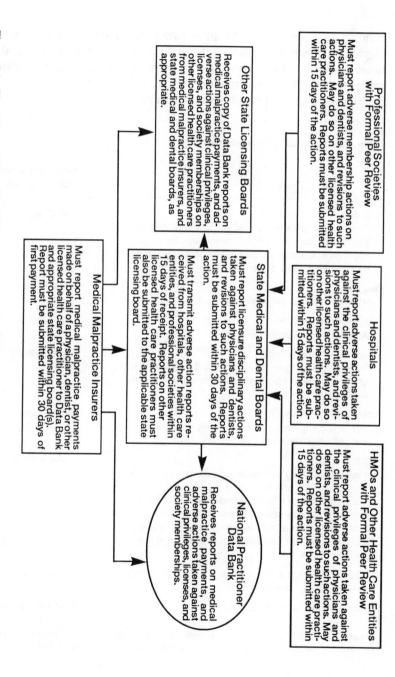

Figure 1-1 Flow Chart of Data Bank Reporting. *Source:* Reprinted from *Guidance for Hospitals and Other Health Care Facilities,* Regional Conference for Hospitals and Other Health Care Entities, by National Practitioner Data Bank, 1990.

conducting peer review, to an attorney (or a person if representing himself or herself) who has filed a malpractice action if the hospital has failed to request Data Bank information, and finally, to any person or entity that requests information that does not identify any particular health care entity or practitioner (see Table 1-2).[16]

Table 1–2 Requesting Information from the Data Bank

Entity	Information Request (Query) Status
Hospitals Screening applicants for medical staff appointment or granting of clinical privileges; every two years for physicians, dentists or other health care practitioners on the medical staff or granted clinical privileges	Must request
Hospitals At other times as they deem necessary	May request
State Licensing Boards At times as they deem necessary	May request
Other Health Care Entities Screening applicants for medical staff appointment or granting of clinical privileges; supporting professional peer review activities	May request
Professional Societies Screening applicants for membership or affiliation; supporting professional peer review activities	May request
Plaintiff's Attorney Plaintiff's attorney or plaintiff representing himself or herself *(pro se)* who has filed a medical malpractice action or claim in a State or Federal court or other adjudicative body against a hospital when evidence is submitted which reveals the hospital failed to query the Data Bank on the practitioner(s) named in the action or claim	May request
Physicians, Dentists, & Other Health Care Practitioners Regarding their own files	May request
Medical Malpractice Insurers	May not request

Source: Reprinted from *Guidance for Hospitals and Other Health Care Facilities*, Regional Conference for Hospitals and Other Health Care Entities, by National Practitioner Data Bank, 1990.

After a medical staff applicant has been granted practice privileges, the hospital must evaluate his or her practice periodically to ensure that patient care is of sufficient quality for reappointment to take place. Information from the federal Data Bank is to be used to supplement this clinical evaluation.

A hospital has a legal duty to patients to use reasonable care in the selection and reappointment of its medical staff. A hospital that fails in this duty can be liable. For example, in *Rule v. Lutheran Hospitals and Homes Society of America*, the parents of an infant sued for injuries sustained by the child during a breech delivery. The family alleged that the hospital failed to investigate the physician's credentials before it granted privileges for certain procedures. In fact, the evidence revealed that the hospital failed to follow the requirements of its own bylaws and conducted only a partial investigation. At trial, testimony revealed that had the hospital made the proper evaluation, it would have determined that the physician was not competent to perform a vaginal breech delivery on a primigravida without supervision. In this case, Mrs. Rule delivered vaginally, but the child suffered from cerebral palsy. A jury found for the plaintiff and awarded $650,000 in damages. The court of appeals affirmed.[17]

Many private physician practices rely on hospitals to do some of the time-consuming physician credential evaluation. Nevertheless, a practice may not delegate all of this responsibility. The practice, at least, should confirm physician licensure, training, and references, and candidates should be interviewed. All the physicians in the practice, whether or not they have been recently hired, should be evaluated periodically. Information for evaluation should be solicited from physician and nonphysician colleagues, and an effort should be made to evaluate clinical outcomes, particularly if several were unexpectedly poor. A practice could be independently liable if it knew or should have known of practice deficiencies such as those in the *Rule* case above.

Nurses should be evaluated in the same general way. Prior to hiring a nurse, a hospital or office should verify that he or she is licensed to practice. This credential assures that the nurse has completed a basic nursing educational program and has passed a standardized nursing examination. Since licensure does not measure skill directly, the prospective employer should require references from instructors, if the nurse is a new graduate, or from the most recent employers. This information should be supplemented by an interview.

After the nurse has been hired, periodic evaluations of performance and behavior should take place. Performance standards should

- set the minimum acceptable behavior for the nurse in accordance with departmental or office standards
- define performance in observable behaviors
- specify the staff nurse role and job description
- include all aspects of the nurse's role, including leadership
- serve as the basis for employee selection and retention[18]

Many nurse managers find it difficult to write honest and complete performance-based evaluations of staff members, especially when the evaluations are not good. From a risk management perspective, however, the failure to evaluate staff properly has two risks. First, an employee who is evaluated as being more skillful than he or she is may be given more responsibility for particular patients than is wise. Second, if the nurse manager feels that the employee should be discharged, there will be inadequate documentation in the personnel file to support that action, and the employee may win an action for wrongful discharge.

More than 3,500 nurse-midwives are certified in the United States. Physician assistants and other types of nurse practitioners also practice in the obstetrics/gynecology specialty to varying degrees. Nurse practitioners, nurse-midwives, nurse-anesthetists, and physician assistants are credentialed through the nursing department, medical staff, or both. Certification for entry into practice is required of both nurse-anesthetists and nurse-midwives and should be confirmed prior to hire. Delineation of practice privileges and the design of standing orders and protocols should accord with state law and with practice standards promulgated by the professions. Nurse-midwives may be hospital employees or may be employed in a private practice and use hospital facilities for aspects of their practices.

The hospital should evaluate qualifications, references, and professional liability insurance of all nonphysician providers who are credentialed as it would any member of its physician staff. Reappointment procedures should be similar to those of physicians, particularly with regard to patient care.

Scope of Practice

Physicians are licensed to practice medicine and surgery, not to practice a particular specialty. However, were a board of medical examiners to determine that the physician consistently practiced in a specialty area for which he or she did not possess credentials, it could discipline the physician. Most physicians, particularly in obstetrics and gynecology, require hospital or surgical center privileges for complete practice. Health care facilities typically restrict physician practice privileges to those services in which a physician can demonstrate training and experience.

State and institutional constraints, along with the threat of professional liability, combine to ensure that most physicians practice within a general professional scope of practice. The boundaries of that practice may change as do the profession and its technology. For example, some obstetricians may be comfortable repairing a bladder during cesarean section; others would prefer to call a urologist in consultation for the repair. Depending on the training and experience of the obstetrician, either could be acceptable.

Nurse-midwives and other nonphysician providers of obstetrical care function under the same types of constraints. Within practice regulation for nurse practitioners, some states have detailed scope of practice statements, while in other states nurse practitioners rely on general statutory and regulatory statements and scope of practice statements promulgated by their trade associations. Nurse practitioners are regulated by state boards of nursing. In the majority of states nurse-midwives are regulated by boards of nursing, but in some states by boards of medicine or departments of health. Every health care provider should be aware of and be guided by applicable state regulations. While the licensee, whether physician or nurse, may not exceed the permissible scope of practice, there is no requirement that every person practice the full scope of the profession for which he or she has trained.

Nursing staffs are licensed and regulated by boards of nursing in the various states. Definitions of nursing practice vary somewhat but are usually very general and provide little guidance for nurses where questions arise about the propriety of nurses assuming particular procedures. Under these circumstances, a nurse must assess the need for a particular procedure, the risks, any training and supervision needed, and relevant institutional factors such as applicable policies and procedures.

Supervision of Practice

Health care providers are not free to practice totally as they wish, at least in a health care facility. The facility has an obligation to provide a mechanism by which physician or nonphysician personnel may bring an example of inadequate or questionable care to the attention of the appropriate authority. Such a mechanism is relatively easy to establish when care is to be reviewed retrospectively. But when a physician makes a health care decision that has immediate implications, such as the decision to discharge a pregnant patient whose fetal monitor strip shows late decelerations, the staff must be able to summon immediate consultation with the authority to override, if necessary, the discharge decision.

Supervision of nurse-midwives, physician assistants, and nurse practitioners is delegated to the specific physician or physicians with whom the nurses or physician assistants have collaboration agreements. If the nurse-midwife is an employee of the hospital, for example, necessary supervision should come from the chief of the service or his or her delegate. A clinical nurse specialist may be supervised by a clinical director within the nursing administration.

Every person who works within a health care facility is responsible to someone, and members of the obstetrical team should have lines of authority clearly established for those rare occasions when they must resort to them. Fortunately, most of the time disputes regarding proper care of a patient can be handled without formal complaints or supervisory mechanisms.

SUMMARY

General principles about risk management provide a background for the more specific risk management recommendations found throughout this book. While the facts will vary, most of the principles can be reduced to three goals of risk management. Occasionally, there is a specific state law or case directly on point that guides choices, such as the reporting of child abuse. In most cases, however, the principles of risk management require that a health care provider make what appears to be the most appropriate and reasonable decision at the time and then document it well.

NOTES

1. T. Goodman, "Risk Management: Why It Became Necessary," *Association of Operating Room Nurses Journal* 39 (1984): 1256.

2. W.P. Keeton, ed., *Prosser and Keeton on Torts,* 5th ed. (St. Paul, Minn.: West Publishing Co., 1984), 1069.

3. *Darling v. Charleston Community Memorial Hospital,* 33 Ill. 2d 326, 211 N.E.2d 253 (1965), cert. denied, 383 U.S. 946 (1966).

4. D. O'Leary, *Background statement: Proposed standards for risk management: Accreditation Manual for Hospitals* (letter accompanying review request dated May 8, 1987).

5. N.Y. Pub. Health Law Section 2805–j(1)(d) and (e) (McKinney Supp. 1988).

6. Conn. Gen. Stat. Section 20–13d (1988).

7. P. Dans, J. Weiner, and S. Otter, "Peer Review Organizations: Promises and Potential Pitfalls," *New England Journal of Medicine* 313 (1985): 1131.

8. 42 USC Section 11101 et seq.

9. K. Steel et al., "Iatrogenic Illness on a General Medical Service at a University Hospital," *New England Journal of Medicine* 304 (12 March 1981): 638–42.

10. I. Press, "The Predisposition to File Claims: The Patient's Perspective," *Law, Medicine & Health Care* 12 (April 1984): 54.

11. Joint Commission on Accreditation of Healthcare Organizations, *Accreditation Manual for Hospitals: 1989* (Chicago: Joint Commission, 1989), 104.

12. Public Law 99–660, Title IV.

13. 42 USC Section 11131(a).

14. Department of Health and Human Services, U.S. Public Health Service, "National Practitioner Data Bank for Adverse Information on Physicians and Other Health Care Providers." *Federal Register* 54 (17 October 1989) Section 60.11: 42722-42734.

15. 42 USC Section 11135(b).

16. Department of Health and Human Services, "National Practitioner Data Bank for Adverse Information on Physicians and Other Health Care Providers."

17. *Rule v. Lutheran Hospitals and Homes Society of America,* 835 F.2d 1250 (8th Cir. 1987).

18. A. Porter, "Assuring Quality through Staff Nurse Performance," *Nursing Clinics of North America* 23 (September 1988): 649.

SUGGESTED READINGS

Chagnon, L., and B. Easterwood. 1986. Managing the risks of obstetrical nursing. *MCN* 11:303–10.

Divoll, M. 1987. The role of the perinatal and neonatal nurse in risk management. *Journal of Perinatal and Neonatal Nursing* 1:1–8.

Purcell, G. 1988. Quality assurance/utilization management and risk management: Deterrents to professional liability. *Clinical Obstetrics and Gynecology* 31:162–68.

Reed, P.A. 1988. Expanding theories of hospital liability: A review. *Journal of Hospital and Health Law* 21 (September): 217.

Southwick, A. 1983. Hospital liability: Two theories have been merged. *Journal of Legal Medicine* 4:1.

Chapter 2

The Professional
Liability System

Law in the United States comes from three general sources. Very basic, but sometimes complex, law arises from constitutions, both state and federal. The second main area is statutory law. State and federal legislatures enact statutes, some of which delegate authority to administrative bodies. For example, it is customary for state legislatures to delegate authority to boards of nursing for the purpose of making regulations for nursing practice. Finally, law is made by judges who decide cases before them. They must interpret statutes and prior decisions in making their determinations. This third type of law is known as common law.

Each state and the federal government maintain separate court systems. All states have trial courts that hear all types of cases. Decisions from trial courts may be appealed on points of law to appeals courts. A new trial is not conducted in an appeals court. Some states have intermediate appeals courts; their opinions may be appealed to each state's highest court. The final judicial arbiter of questions of state law is the highest state court (unless federal questions are raised, in which case the matter may be appealed to the U.S. Supreme Court). States use different names for their courts; the names do not predictably indicate the level of the court. For example, the highest state court in Connecticut is called the supreme court, while in New York, the supreme court is the trial court.

At the federal level, the trial court is called the district court. Appeals are taken to the court of appeals for the relevant area (called the circuit).

A final appeal may be taken to the U.S. Supreme Court, most of whose jurisdiction is discretionary. A decision by the U.S. Supreme Court on a point of law is binding on all U.S. courts.

In general, a tort is a civil, as opposed to a criminal, wrong (other than a breach of contract action) for which the law provides a remedy in damages.[1] The negligence claim, which became a separate action during the early part of the nineteenth century, falls within the tort category. The development of the negligence doctrine coincided with the industrial revolution and may have been stimulated by an increase in the number of industrial accidents and development of the railroads.[2] At around that time, lawsuits alleging intentional acts began to be grouped as one type of action and negligence remained the main basis for unintentional civil wrongs. Today, negligence is the most common cause of action for accidental injury.

Negligence actions have arisen primarily from the common law rather than from statutes. While there are a few statutes defining aspects of negligence actions, such as statutes of limitation, most of the definition of the negligence case has evolved in opinions written by judges in individual cases. Trial court decisions or jury verdicts are often reported in the media, but few written opinions are published. Legal decisions that act as precedents for later court cases are written and later published in a national reporter system. Written opinions are often issued by appeals courts, but only a small percentage of cases actually brought are eventually reported as written appellate opinions.

The precedents established by written opinions allow each state (and negligence law varies somewhat from state to state) to develop a body of law to be used by the courts in deciding similar questions. The principle of stare decisis holds that decisions on points of law made by higher courts must be followed by lower courts subject to that jurisdiction. While state courts often look to decisions in other states when facing a question of first impression, no principle requires that the states have parallel views on the same questions in tort law.

The malpractice, or professional liability, action is one type of negligence action. A malpractice action can be brought against health care providers, but increasingly other professions are becoming involved in this type of action. Malpractice actions have been brought against lawyers, accountants, dentists, chiropractors, hairdressers, and other licensed and unlicensed professionals.

Under the legal system of the United States, the ancient doctrine of sovereign immunity protects the government from suit unless it has given its permission. However, federal sovereign immunity has been abrogated to some extent in this country by the Federal Tort Claims Act. This act gave congressional permission for actions brought against the federal government that involve the negligent conduct of government employees. Under this statute, those (other than active military personnel) who wish to bring an action for malpractice by federal employees acting within the scope of their employment (as in a Veterans Administration hospital) must sue the United States of America. Certain types of actions, including those for libel and slander, are not permitted by statute. Individual defendants may not be named in the action; trial is to a judge without a jury.[3] In most cases, the Federal Tort Claims Act is the exclusive remedy for malpractice against members of the military.

The U.S. Supreme Court has held in the so-called *Feres* doctrine that active duty service personnel are barred from suing the United States for negligence under the Federal Tort Claims Act.[4] While the *Feres* doctrine has come under attack in subsequent cases, it has not been overturned.

ELEMENTS OF A MALPRACTICE ACTION

Four elements of a malpractice action must be proved by a preponderance of the evidence before the plaintiff can prevail. They are duty, breach of duty, causation, and damages.

The duty to use reasonable care in medicine and nursing arises from the health care provider-patient relationship. Ordinarily, there must be such a relationship for a malpractice case to arise. The fact of the relationship may be disputed, but usually it is not. For example, a relationship is established, for all practical purposes, whenever a nurse within the scope of employment undertakes the care of a patient, even for just a moment.

The plaintiff must show that the defendants failed to conform to the duty established by the fact of the nurse-patient relationship. The standard of care is generally set by what a reasonable person with similar

138,040

training and experience, while acting under the same or similar circumstances, would have done. This rule has been codified in some states. For example, a Connecticut statute passed in 1987 provides that the

> prevailing professional standard of care for a given health care provider shall be that level of care, skill, and treatment which, in light of all relevant surrounding circumstances, is recognized as acceptable and appropriate by reasonably prudent similar health care providers.[5]

Precisely what the standard is within the particular case, and whether it was breached, is usually the subject of expert testimony (except in cases where the injury is a nontechnical type known to the layman). There may be cases where the standard of care itself is not disputed. For example, most nurses would agree on the proper placement of a gluteal intramuscular injection in the context of an alleged sciatic nerve injury. In other cases, the standard of care may be subject to considerable dispute.

The failure by the nurse to conform to the applicable standard of care must be shown to be a proximate cause of the damage suffered by the patient. The injuries must have been reasonable and foreseeable consequences of the defendant's acts and omissions. In some cases causation is not disputed, while in others there is considerable disagreement over whether the nursing error in question was related at all to the patient's outcome.

Finally, the plaintiff must show damages even though they may be small. A small injury or compensable loss simply reduces the amount of the recovery; it does not bar the case. Usually the patient must show physical injury before he or she can recover money for noneconomic damages, generally referred to as pain and suffering or emotional distress.

There are cases where the negligent or intentional infliction of emotional distress has been alleged, but without any physical injury. In some of these cases, recovery has been permitted. For example, in *Johnson v. Woman's Hospital*[6] the parents of a premature infant arranged for the hospital to handle the disposition of fetal remains after the infant's death.

The mother was discharged and returned to her physician six weeks later. At that postpartum visit, she inquired about the disposition of the infant. She was escorted to the hospital by a member of the doctor's staff. Upon her arrival, a hospital employee opened a refrigerator and handed the mother a jar containing the discolored and shriveled body of the baby. Subsequently, the mother suffered nightmares and required psychiatric treatment. The mother and her husband sued the hospital and physician for outrageous conduct in displaying the body of the infant floating in the jar. They recovered a verdict of $300,000, but it was reduced by the judge to $175,000. On appeal, the judgment against the physician was dismissed but upheld against the hospital. The court held that the hospital, through its employee, intended to display the baby to the mother and that this conduct was sufficiently outrageous to allow the award of damages for emotional injury even though there was no physical injury.

Since it is not possible to restore the patient to his or her predamaged state, damages requested are monetary. As a practical matter, this requires that any type of injury, from death or loss of vision to scarring, must be valued in dollars. Compensatory damages include both economic and noneconomic damages. Economic damages are those awarded for loss of past and projected future earnings, past and projected medical expenses, and other out-of-pocket costs. Noneconomic damages are awards for pain and suffering.

Punitive damages, designed to punish the defendants for some type of egregious conduct, may be awarded in medical malpractice actions. They are claimed often in some states, but seldom in others. The money awarded as punitive damages is often not insurable. In some states punitive damages are limited to attorney's fees, while in others the amount of damages is unlimited.

In addition to defenses involving the failure of the plaintiff to prove all of the elements required for proof of malpractice, the law provides other defenses that can be used in a malpractice action. One is the doctrine of contributory negligence, which is no longer used in many jurisdictions today. This harsh rule held that if the plaintiff was in any way negligent, all recovery against the defendant was barred. In the place of contributory negligence, many courts and legislatures have substituted so-called comparative negligence. Under this rule, the negligence of the patient (for example, by not following postdischarge directions) is weighed against the negligence of the health care provider. One of several formulas may be used to allow the patient to recover the total monetary amount minus that percentage attributable to his or her own fault.

A health care defendant can also defend a case by alleging that the plaintiff knowingly and voluntarily (without coercion) assumed any risk involved in the treatment. Good documentation about discussions with the patient is clearly necessary to prevail in this defense. Finally, a case may be barred, regardless of its merits, if suit is not filed within the applicable statute of limitations.

TYPES OF MALPRACTICE LIABILITY

For the purposes of discussing malpractice actions, there are three general types of liability: vicarious, corporate, and personal. In the *Johnson* case above, the hospital was vicariously liable for the conduct of its employee under the doctrine of respondeat superior. This doctrine makes an employer liable for the civil wrongs of its employee who is acting within the scope of his or her employment. Where there is vicarious liability, it is not alleged that the employer itself acted improperly, merely that it is liable vicariously for the acts of its employees.

The second type of liability is corporate liability. In the context of a malpractice case there may be allegations that the hospital hired and retained an incompetent nurse or physician, who then acted improperly. This is not an allegation of vicarious liability but instead is an accusation that the hospital was actively negligent in its hiring and retention practices. Damages can be awarded for this type of negligence in addition to any recoverable damages for vicarious liability.

Finally, a party can be personally liable by reason of being named as a defendant. The term "personal liability" is often confusing. It can mean simply that one is a defendant, or it can mean that there is no insurance applicable and, therefore, the defendant must pay any judgment out of personal assets. It also can mean that a professional must be responsible for his or her own acts in law whether or not there is insurance to pay any damages awarded.

OTHER LIABILITY CASES

Most claims made against health care professionals belong in the general category of malpractice, but other types of claims also may be filed against them. These claims may involve informed consent, wrongful conception, wrongful birth, or wrongful life; false imprisonment; or defamation of character. Some of these claims are variations on the usual malpractice case.

Informed Consent Claims

Although the doctrine of informed consent did not appear until the 1950s, there were earlier cases in which courts affirmed a patient's right to refuse uninvited care. For example, in the 1905 case of *Pratt v. Davis*,[7] Mrs. Pratt consulted Dr. Davis who was considered an authority on the treatment of epilepsy, a condition from which she had suffered for many years. Dr. Davis concluded that a total abdominal hysterectomy was indicated. He performed the surgery after telling Mrs. Pratt that cervical lacerations would be repaired. The lawsuit that followed was brought as a battery action, and the claim was made that the surgery was done without consent. During the case Dr. Pratt argued that "when a patient places herself in the care of a surgeon for treatment without [express limitations] upon his authority, she thereby in law consents that he may perform such operations as in his best judgment is proper and essential to her welfare." The court found Dr. Pratt liable for battery and held that the physician may not "violate without permission the bodily integrity of his patient."

Gradually during the 1950s, judges began to inquire about whether patients might be entitled both to consent to the treatment the physician proposed and to decide whether the risks, benefits, and alternatives were justified. Physicians then would be required to disclose this information to their patients, a practice that was not customary at that time.

The first case in which the doctrine of informed consent appeared was *Salgo v. Leland Stanford Jr. University Board of Trustees*.[8] Mr. Salgo alleged that he suffered permanent paraplegia as a result of the negligent performance of translumbar aortography done at Stanford University Hospital. Since he could not claim that he had not consented to the procedure at all (the elements of a battery action), he claimed in the lawsuit that the physicians had negligently failed to inform him of the risks inherent in the procedure. The court's opinion, which was somewhat confusing and certainly stimulated discussion both within and without the medical profession, stated that the physician must not withhold "any facts which are necessary to form the basis of an intelligent consent by the patient." The judge went on to limit this broad standard by indicating that the physician must exercise discretion in providing the information.

After this early case and a few subsequent actions, standards for, as well as exceptions to, disclosure for obtaining informed consent were at least somewhat apparent. In the various state courts that have addressed consent questions, three standards for disclosure have appeared. The first is called the "professional" standard. In these cases, the standard of disclosure by which the defendant physician is judged is the same as in other aspects of malpractice law: what a physician with similar training and experience and under the circumstances would disclose. This standard has been criticized, because it permits physicians to decide how much or how little to tell patients.

The second standard is the "subjective" standard, in which the patient is permitted to testify retrospectively about whether he or she would have undergone the procedure if information about the complication that has already been experienced had been known at the time of the procedure. This standard has been criticized, because it permits patients to change their minds in retrospect.

The third standard has been called the "reasonable person" or objective standard. In this type of case, there must be testimony about what a reasonable person in the plaintiff's position would have wanted if the potential risks, benefits, and alternatives had been fully disclosed. As an example, in *Marshall v. University of Chicago Hospitals and Clinics*, a woman brought an action against a surgeon alleging, after a failed tubal ligation, that she was not told of a possible one percent failure rate. She claimed that she would have preferred to take birth control pills although they had a ten percent failure rate and made her sick. The court found this argument unpersuasive and stated that the only reasonable inference "from the objective evidence is that a reasonable person in plaintiff's position would not have refused the tubal ligation under the circumstances." This holding was further bolstered by the fact that the patient, after the birth of the unexpected child and by then well aware of the failure rate in tubal ligations, chose to have another tubal ligation four months prior to filing suit.[9]

While an occasional case is brought as an informed consent case only, that is, claiming that the surgery was done properly but that there was not consent, it is now more common to find claims about the adequacy of the consent appended to a general malpractice case as an additional allegation.

Wrongful Conception, Wrongful Birth, and Wrongful Life Claims

Wrongful conception, wrongful birth, and wrongful life claims are forms of malpractice actions named to suggest the types of claims being made. Wrongful conception claims are generally made after a sterilization procedure has failed and an unplanned pregnancy later occurs. Usually, the claim is for the birth of the child, not that the child was unloved or defective. These actions are permitted in the United States, but there is considerable dispute over what damages should be permitted. Should the negligent physician pay for the entire costs of rearing a child since the child was unplanned, should the physician pay for nothing, or should the entire costs be reduced by some value equal to the "benefits" that a child provides a family? The courts have split on these questions.

Wrongful birth claims, also permitted in the United States, are brought by parents against physicians. In an example of this type of case, the child is usually defective and the parents claim either that preconception counseling or genetics advice was faulty or that, after the conception, prenatal diagnosis was inadequate. In the first situation, the parents had relied on the faulty advice and conceived; in the second, the parents could have chosen an abortion but did not do so because they were reassured by the physician.

Wrongful life cases, permitted in only a few states, are actions brought by the child (represented by the parent or guardian). They are usually brought in conjunction with wrongful birth allegations. In wrongful life cases, the claim on behalf of the child is that the child would have been better off never having been born and that the birth was due to the negligent conduct of the physician. Courts have usually rejected these claims, because they find themselves unable to place a value on a life that would have been better off if not experienced. In effect, the court would have to value death over life.

Wrongful life and wrongful birth cases are discussed more thoroughly in Chapter 6.

False Imprisonment Claims

In the context of professional liability, false imprisonment claims are often those of improper restraint. This type of claim is based on the patient either being kept in the hospital improperly over his or her objections or being placed in mechanical restraints unnecessarily. Both of these actions generally occur in the context of emergency service or psychiatric care but also may occur in other areas less frequently. A false imprisonment claim can be cast in the form of a negligence action, but traditionally it has been seen as an intentional tort. The patient claims damages to personal liberty, and usually emotional distress is also claimed.

Defamation of Character Claims

Defamation of character is not often related to professional liability, but the allegations in this type of action can result in a professional liability claim. An action for defamation of character claims damage to an individual's good name or reputation via libel or slander. Libel is defamation by the written word; slander is spoken. In both cases, the damaging information must be communicated to a third party or "published." An insulting comment directed to another person may give rise to an action for the intentional infliction of emotional distress, but unless the remark is communicated to a third party there will be no defamation.

The law of defamation is rather complex generally, but ways in which claims are made in the professional liability context are not. Defamation claims have been made against physicians who disclosed confidential medical information. These claims are usually not successful, because truthful information disclosed in good faith will generally relieve the defendant of liability for any damage to reputation. Of course, there may be other ways to find liability for the improper disclosure of confidential information. Health care professionals also can become involved in defamation actions through their ill-considered comments, particularly about a business, that are quoted in the press. Health care providers should be careful not to comment on subjects about which they have insufficient knowledge; even if they comment only on appropriate topics, they must be sure that reporters understand what they say.

Some commentators have speculated that defamation claims may be brought as part of an action alleging that a patient's human immunodeficiency virus (HIV) status was reported to a third party, and that the third party should not have been told or that the third party was given the incorrect result. HIV carriers have suffered stigmatization, along with loss of jobs and housing, so dissemination of an incorrect (presumably a false positive) result could clearly generate provable damages. It is even possible that damages need not be proven, although this remains to be seen. In the old law of slander, an exception to proof of damage was made for certain "loathsome" diseases that were thought to be permanent, lingering, and incurable.[10]

OBSTETRICAL CLAIMS

Aggregated information on obstetrical professional liability case frequency (the number of cases) and severity (what it costs to pay the claims) is difficult to determine, because insurance companies do not generally share their data. Many authorities believe that, until recently, claims rates have been rising. Certainly, patients seem more aware of their legal rights today and more likely at least to question unfavorable outcomes. In one analysis, close to one-half of patients surveyed considered as errors such things as minor residual problems after major lifesaving treatment or unsightly scarring after emergency surgery.[11]

The American College of Obstetricians and Gynecologists (ACOG) published in 1988 its third biennial national survey of the impact of professional liability on its members. Data from 1,984 responding members indicate that 70.6 percent of the physicians who responded to the survey had had at least one professional liability claim filed against them during their medical careers. Of the respondents, 25.1 percent had had one claim filed; 20 percent, two claims; 12 percent, three claims; and 13.5 percent, four or more claims. The average number of claims filed against obstetricians/gynecologists responding to the survey was 1.7. In District II of ACOG, which includes New York and Bermuda, nearly 30 percent of responding physicians had had four or more claims filed against them during their medical careers.

Of the total claims reported in the ACOG survey, 52 percent were obstetrical and 48 percent gynecological. Brain damage to the infant was the primary allegation in 30.9 percent of the obstetrical claims. Infant and maternal deaths were the primary allegations in 14.7 percent and 6.5 percent, respectively. In the obstetrical cases on which the claims were based, the physicians reported that electronic fetal monitoring was used in 45.8 percent, oxytocic agents in 21.8 percent, and forceps in 17.3 percent. Postmaturity accounted for 10.5 percent of the claims. Breech presentation problems were present in 6.4 percent of the cases.

The ACOG respondents reported 495 claims in which some payment had been made on behalf of a physician through settlement, arbitration, or jury verdict. The average payment for obstetrical claims was $221,379 (compared with an average of $63,903 for gynecological claims). Payments of $1 million or more occurred in 3.8 percent of the cases.[12]

Data from the Risk Management Foundation of the Harvard Medical Institutions showed that 43 percent of their cases concerned obstetrics. Of all obstetrics cases, 17 percent contained allegations of failure to identify, or delay in identification of, fetal distress during the intrapartum period. Regarding payments, 38 percent of the money paid on all types of obstetrical claims involved this group of 17 percent, which indicated they were more expensive than the other claims analyzed.[13]

Typically, birth injury claims are among the most expensive to settle. Otherwise normal infants who are injured by improper care at birth may suffer lifelong damages, often without a decrease in life expectancy. High medical costs may include the expense of institutional care for life. There may be special education costs and expenses for prosthetic devices, plus the predictable future loss of income. These costs are only for economic damages. An award for the loss of life's enjoyment or pain and suffering, in those jurisdictions that permit this type of award, may also result in substantial additional payments.

CONDUCT OF A PROFESSIONAL LIABILITY ACTION

How a Claim Is Made

A professional liability claim against a health care provider may be made by letter or by lawsuit. In the first instance, the attorney for the patient (or infrequently the patient) writes a letter to the hospital, physician, nurse, or other potential defendant stating the plaintiff's intent to claim damages for personal injuries. The letter typically advises the recipient to forward it to the applicable insurance carrier.

The second way to make a claim is by filing suit. In this case, the first notice received by a health care provider that he or she has been named as a defendant is service of process from a sheriff or process server. In some areas, a copy of the lawsuit may be left at the defendant's residence without actual personal service.

Evaluation and Defense of a Claim

Upon receiving notice, the health care provider should immediately forward the letter or suit papers to the insurance carrier responsible for defending the claim. The claim material should be hand-carried or sent by certified mail. Failure to forward notice of a claim promptly may prejudice the ultimate defense of the claim, and the insurance carrier may deny coverage. Relevant medical records should be sent with the notice of claim or immediately thereafter.

If the claim has been made by letter, the insurer will evaluate its substance, as well as the medical records and information from the insured, and respond. At times, an insurer will be able to settle an appropriate claim before the institution of a lawsuit. This will save costs for all parties. If the insurer refuses to settle this way, it will so notify the claimant, who will then decide whether to drop the claim or to file suit.

When suit is filed, the insurer will retain an attorney for the insured defendant. The defendant should meet with the attorney early in the case to ensure that the attorney has access to appropriate information about the claim. Later in the course of the legal proceedings, the defendant may assist in any response to questions from the plaintiff (interrogatories) and may be required to give a deposition (pretrial sworn testimony). Other health care professionals involved in the case and the plaintiff also may have their depositions taken. Any witness in a malpractice action should have reviewed the relevant medical records prior to deposition so that the testimony given in response to questions is accurate and truthful. Deposition testimony is transcribed. In some jurisdictions, it is customary for the deponent to receive, correct, and sign the transcript of the deposition. This should be done with care, since a deposition transcript can be used later at trial to impair the credibility of a witness whose testimony has changed.

It will be necessary for the defense to retain one or more expert witnesses. The defendant may be asked whether he or she knows of suitable experts. The defendant should not personally contact these professionals, because such conversations are discoverable in litigation. Once experts are disclosed for either side, it is customary to take their depositions. The defendant is not required to be present at the depositions taken during the case, but he or she is entitled to be present. For tactical reasons, the defense attorney may ask the defendant to attend one or more depositions. The plaintiff may also attend.

Although depositions may take place pursuant to subpoena, ordinarily they are scheduled for the convenience of all parties. Health care defendants find it frustrating that a scheduled deposition is often canceled with very little notice from the canceling party. Although most depositions take only a few hours, occasionally a deposition may be continued and last for more than a day. If this occurs, a subsequent day of testimony is also scheduled in advance.

At any time during the course of the case, settlement discussions may take place. If settlement does not occur, however, at completion of preparations the case will go to trial, usually in front of a jury. Most defense attorneys believe that it is useful to have the defendants in the courtroom for most of the trial. A trial can last from just a few hours to several weeks. The case may settle during trial proceedings; otherwise the jury will return its verdict. An appeal can be taken by either side after final judgment in the case.

Settlement of a Claim

Most professional liability cases settle with or without payment prior to the conclusion of a trial and often before the trial begins. Questions about tactics in the case should arise early in the claims process. A defendant may prefer that the case be settled because of the belief that his or her judgment during the incident could have been better. This opinion should be made clear to defense counsel early in the case so that settlement efforts can be made. However, it is not always possible to settle a case for a reasonable amount without considerable time spent by the defendant and others, and occasionally a case of this kind must go to trial because the plaintiff's demand is considered unreasonable.

In other cases, the defendant may believe that his or her conduct is defensible and that the case should be defended. Although many insurance policies do not give the defendant the right to prevent a settlement, most insurers do consider the wishes of the defendant. Before making a settlement recommendation, however, those working on behalf of the defense will review the medical records for gaps or inconsistencies in documentation, examine relevant medical literature, and consult an expert informally to be sure that the defendant's position is credible. If a case is to go to trial, the defendant must be willing to expend time and effort to assist in preparation of the case and must be present at the trial. By using this information, plus assessments of the plaintiff, the defendant's appearance as a potential witness, and the damages claimed by the plaintiff, the defense will informally estimate the likelihood that the defense will prevail at trial and the potential jury verdict if it does not prevail. These admittedly imprecise calculations are used to judge any demand made by the plaintiff. As a final imponderable, the insurer may select a favorable case for trial even if the matter could be settled for a small amount, especially if the plaintiff's attorney sues repeatedly for the same types of alleged injuries. In such cases, the insurer may believe that a defense verdict will deter similar cases.

The willing and confident participation of the defendant in the case from its inception can be more important than any other factor to ensure that his or her views prevail in the determination of the outcome of the case. Insurers are more conscious than ever that settlements on behalf of defendants are not without lasting effects. The settlement may be reportable to state and now federal (under the Health Care Quality Improvement Act of 1986) authorities, to other insurers from whom the defendant may seek professional liability insurance, and to hospitals when the physician seeks clinical privileges or their renewal.

PROFESSIONAL LIABILITY INSURANCE

Professional liability insurance, like all forms of insurance, is a risk-sharing device; that is, those desiring to participate join the group, and losses are spread within the group. Most health care professionals carry insurance in order to insulate their personal assets from the possibility of large judgments against them. An uninsured nurse, for example, who is sued must pay defense costs immediately at an hourly rate. If there is a settlement or jury verdict, wages may be garnished, liens can be placed on real estate and other assets, and some assets can be sold. Insurance, by contrast, pays defense costs and any judgment up to the policy limits. This partially insulates the professional's family and personal property.

Although most states do not require health care professionals to carry insurance, hospitals generally require their staffs to be insured. Usually the hospital insures its employees, but it also requires its nonemployed medical staff (including credentialed nonphysicians such as nurse-midwives and nurse practitioners) to carry adequate amounts of liability insurance. Some hospitals specify the amounts considered minimally acceptable for their staffs. There have been court cases challenging these hospital requirements as unreasonable, but hospitals have prevailed.

Nurses can be insured through their employer, individually, or both. Employer-provided insurance has two specific advantages. First, it is usually offered as a benefit of employment at no cost to the employee. Second, when it is provided by a hospital, the amounts of applicable insurance are usually higher than an individual would choose, or perhaps even could afford, to purchase alone. High levels of insurance that hospitals often carry for their employees may not be available to an individual nurse for purchase at any price. Disadvantages include the fact that employer-provided insurance is applicable only during the scope of employment with that employer, and it does not insure a nurse during practice in another setting unless the employer sends the nurse there as part of his or her employment.

A nurse can choose to purchase professional liability insurance personally, and many do as long as the premium costs remain reasonable. Insurance premiums for nurses have been rising as they have been for other professionals. The policy will cover the nurse where he or she chooses to practice (subject to any exclusions in the policy, usually for nurse-midwifery and nurse anesthesia). The policy generally states that it is not primarily applicable if there is other primary insurance (this may be the case where a nurse is sued as an employee of a hospital that carries insurance for such instances). A private policy also will not permit the nurse to select a lawyer. The insurance company will hire an attorney with whom it is familiar. Finally, a private policy may not mean that the nurse can block a settlement that he or she opposes. Usually an insurance company will consult its insured about a proposed settlement, but most policies do not permit the insured to prevent a settlement. Some insurers permit an insured to refuse any settlement, but if a settlement is approved the insurance company controls the amount.

There are two types of professional liability insurance now available: occurrence and claims-made. In most places physicians cannot purchase occurrence policies, but many nursing policies of this type are still available. Private insurance for nurse-midwives, however, is now of the claims-made type.

Occurrence policies insure the period when the incident took place and will cover a claim based on that incident no matter when it is brought. For example, if the incident took place in 1980 but the suit was not filed until 1990, the 1980 occurrence policy will cover the claim. For this reason, old policies of the occurrence type should be retained by the insured nurse.

Claims-made policies work somewhat differently. Each policy is applicable for a year and covers only claims brought during that policy year. Claims made on incidents that occurred during earlier years with the same company also will be covered. However, if the insured wishes to stop practice and stop paying premiums, there is no coverage for claims brought in later years. To cover such claims, the insured must purchase a reporting endorsement, or "tail" policy. This one-time premium will cover all claims brought in later years on incidents that occurred during the years covered by the insurance company. In effect, a reporting endorsement converts a claims-made policy into an occurrence policy.

If an insured wishes to switch to a different professional liability insurance company (for example, one with less expensive rates), there may be two choices available. First, the insured can purchase a reporting endorsement from the original company. The insured will then pay less expensive claims-made premiums to the second company. Claims-made premiums start low and rise over a period of five years (at the end of five years, the premiums are equivalent to what an occurrence policy would cost). In the second choice, the insured, with the consent of the second company, may pay higher than base rates with the second company agreeing to provide "prior acts" coverage. In effect, this is a reporting endorsement.

Insurance is purchased in specified amounts and may be expressed as $X/$X. The first amount is the per-claim amount; the insurance company will pay no more than that amount per claim in any one insurance year. This amount usually includes costs of defense. The second number is the aggregate amount and expresses the maximum total amount the insurance company will pay for claims made during that year, no matter how many claims are made against the insured. Thus, if the numbers are $1 million/$3 million and a judgment is rendered in one claim for $1.5 million, the company will pay only the $1 million for that claim. It will, however, pay many smaller claims during the policy year up to a total of $3 million.

CONSEQUENCES OF A MALPRACTICE CLAIM

Two types of professional consequences may result from a malpractice claim: employment-related and license-related. If an incident, for example, that occurs at a hospital, is one that demonstrates unusual carelessness by a nurse or is just one more in a series of incidents involving the same nurse, the hospital may choose to begin the process of internal discipline or termination of employment. Discipline should be the result of poor performance or behavior and is usually completed by the time any malpractice claim is brought.

Some states, such as New York, require that a hospital must file a report in substantial detail when any incident results in harm to a patient. A nurse involved in this type of incident will be included in the state investigation of the incident. In states that do not have reporting requirements, hospitals conduct their own internal investigations of such incidents.

A few states require that insurers that pay more than a specified amount of money on behalf of an insured report that fact to the relevant licensing board in the state. The board may then investigate and decide if any disciplinary action is warranted. In most states, however, the licensing boards, including the nursing boards, receive most of their complaints from members of the public. All states have statutes that list general grounds for nurse discipline. These statutes may include language covering negligence, gross negligence, repeated malpractice, or malpractice. A nursing board may learn of possible malpractice and investigate the incident, but it is unusual for a professional license to be suspended or revoked for one error, unless the error is extremely egregious or the harm was provoked intentionally. For example, disciplinary actions have been brought against nurses who intentionally disconnected ventilatory support without a physician's order.

When a licensee is investigated by a licensing board, the licensee is entitled to be informed of the charges and to have adequate due process. If the board decides to recommend discipline (usually a censure, suspension, or revocation of a license), the licensee can challenge the decision in court or can agree to it. The costs of mounting a defense to a license action are not covered by professional liability insurance.

The requirements of the Health Care Quality Improvement Act of 1986 are discussed in Chapter 1. The act requires that an insurer or self-insured hospital report to the National Practitioner Data Bank about malpractice settlements and judgments on behalf of any licensed health care provider.[14]

TORT REFORM

Most of the professional liability system is not statutory, but some portions are (even nonstatutory rules can be "law"). In recent years there has been considerable discussion about altering even some of the nonstatutory rules through legislative action. If these changes are made, all professional liability claims will be affected.

Discussion of tort reform has centered on caps for noneconomic damages, abolition of joint and several liability, statutes of limitation, and other modifications in the tort system, including recently the limited use of a no-fault system.

Cap on Noneconomic Damages

Noneconomic damages, as indicated previously, are awarded for other than out-of-pocket expenses suffered or reasonably predicted for the future. These damages may include mental anguish, pain, and suffering. A cap on noneconomic damages creates an upper limit on the amount a jury can award for damages that may be viewed as speculative. Several states have passed this type of legislation for medical malpractice cases. Some courts have found the caps unconstitutional, while others have upheld them. For example, a $250,000 cap on noneconomic damages was upheld by the California Supreme Court as constitutional.[15]

Several decisions have invalidated laws that attempted to place caps on total damages (including economic and noneconomic). Courts in these cases have been influenced by concerns that a plaintiff might not be able to recover even the total provable medical expenses.

Abolition of Joint and Several Liability

In most states, the rule of joint and several liability means that a plaintiff who sues several defendants and wins can recover the full amount of the award from any of the defendants. Thus, a plaintiff can recover a jury verdict of $1 million from an insured defendant who was found to have only 10 percent of responsibility for the incident. In many, but not all, states the defendant who is forced to pay the entire judgment could sue the codefendants for contribution to the payment, but if those defendants are insolvent or immune from suit, there is no practical way to recover the money.

Some states have abolished the rule and replaced it with one of "several liability." Under this rule, the plaintiff recovers from the defendants according to their percentage of fault for the injury. Plaintiffs may argue that the rule of several liability forces a plaintiff, who had no fault for the injury (or if there was fault, the recovery has been reduced by an amount considered equal to plaintiff's fault) to absorb the financial loss if any of the defendants are unable to pay, and that joint and several liability is preferable from the injured plaintiff's perspective.

The rule of joint and several liability is one reason why hospitals began to require their professional staffs to carry specific amounts of professional liability insurance. Under this rule, if the nonemployed physician and the hospital are sued together and the physician has no insurance or assets (the physician may have transferred all personal assets to a family member before suit was brought), the hospital is forced to pay the total judgment even if its personnel are barely at fault. Insurance requirements for staff minimize this threat to hospital financial well-being.

Statutes of Limitation

In each state, a statute of limitation sets the period of time within which a suit must be filed against a defendant if it is to be brought at all. The statute begins to run at the time of the negligent act or, in some states, at the time the negligent act reasonably could have been discovered. The time set by the statute does not run if the plaintiff is incompetent, if there has been fraudulent concealment by the defendant (for example, a hospital knew that a sponge had been left in the plaintiff after surgery but did not tell the plaintiff), or, traditionally, if the plaintiff is a minor. In jurisdictions that follow the traditional protective rule for minors, the statute of limitations does not begin to run until the child reaches the age of majority. Then the statute runs as it would for any injury. This can mean that 21 years can elapse between the injury and the lawsuit.

Many states have changed the traditional application of statutes of limitations to minors. The changes are not consistent. Some states have decided that the general malpractice statute of limitation will be applicable to birth injuries and no exception has been made, while others have chosen an intermediate age (such as six or eight years of age) to toll the statute. Some commentators who argue in favor of tort reform believe that the statute of limitation for minors should be at age eight, for example, since by then any injury a child has suffered at birth should be quite evident.[16]

Other Tort System Modifications

Commentators have argued that the tort system is flawed in many ways, but there had been no serious movement to change the system until professional liability insurance premiums became very expensive for some types of practice. At least partly because of exorbitant insurance premiums, some obstetricians, for example, have chosen to stop practicing obstetrics.[17]

Other changes that have been discussed in some states have included modification of the contingency system by which most plaintiffs' attorneys are paid throughout the United States. There is no serious suggestion that the contingency fee system will be abolished, because in many cases the system allows patients to sue who could not afford to pay hourly attorney fees. Some states have limited the percentage of the recovery payable to the plaintiff's attorney as the amount of recovery increases.

Some states also have enacted statutes to establish malpractice screening panels that hear cases before they enter the legal system. While the findings of such panels are not binding on the parties, the results can be admissible at a later trial. Most of these systems have been held constitutional. In those cases where courts have found constitutional defects, the problems involved impermissible delays or connecting the use of the panel to the right to jury trial (which is guaranteed by many constitutions).

No-Fault Compensation

In 1987, Virginia became the first state to enact a statute that provides reimbursement for a limited category of neurologically devastated infants without regard to the fault of the provider. The Virginia Birth-related Neurological Injury Compensation Act defines the injury as an

"injury to the brain or spinal cord of an infant caused by the deprivation of oxygen or mechanical injury occurring in the course of labor, delivery or resuscitation in the immediate post-delivery period in a hospital which renders the infant permanently nonambulatory, aphasic, incontinent, and in need of assistance in all phases of daily living."[18]

This statute went into effect on January 1, 1988. If the infant qualifies under the above definition, no proof of provider negligence is required for compensation. In return, these children and their families may not sue for recovery under the traditional tort system.[19]

Florida also has established a no-fault compensation system for birth-related neurological injuries, which went into effect on January 1, 1989. This statute has a slightly broader definition for inclusion of infants for coverage.[20]

The success of these laws remains to be seen. As of January 1, 1990, no infant had sought coverage under either law.[21]

SUMMARY

This chapter provides only an outline of the complexities of the professional liability system. Tort systems are governed by state laws, and these laws vary among the states. For example, every health care provider should be aware of the statute of limitation in his or her state. Proposed changes in tort law are usually discussed in local newspapers. Professional health care providers should follow evolution of the tort law, because it can substantially affect their practices.

NOTES

1. W.P. Keeton, ed., *Prosser and Keeton on Torts*, 5th ed. (St. Paul, Minn.: West Publishing Co., 1984), 3.

2. Ibid., 161.

3. 28 USC 2671–2680.

4. *Fares, Executrix v. United States*, 340 U.S. 135 (1950).

5. Conn. Gen. Stat. Section 52–184c.

6. *Johnson v. Woman's Hospital*, 527 S.W. 2d 133 (Tenn. 1975).

7. *Pratt v. Davis*, 118 Ill. App. 161 (1905).

8. *Salgo v. Leland Stanford Jr. University Board of Trustees*, 317 P.2d 170 (Cal. Dist. Ct. App. 1957).

9. *Marshall v. University of Chicago Hospitals and Clinics*, 520 N.E.2d 740 (Ill. App. 1 Dist. 1987).

10. Keeton, *Prosser and Keeton on Torts*, 790.

11. I. Press, "The Predisposition to File Claims: The Patient's Perspective," *Law, Medicine & Health Care* 12 (April 1984): 53.

12. American College of Obstetricians and Gynecologists, *Professional Liability and Its Effects: Report of a 1987 Survey of ACOG's Membership* (Washington, D.C.: ACOG, March 1988).

13. Risk Management Foundation, "Fetal Monitoring Problems during Labor Associated with Most Serious OB Claims," *Forum* 7 (March–June 1986): 19.

14. Public Law 99-660, Title IV.

15. *Fein v. Kaiser Permanente*, 695 P.2d 665 (Cal. 1985), appeal dismissed, 106 S.Ct. 214 (1985).

16. American Hospital Association, *Medical Malpractice Task Force Report on Tort Reform and Compendium of Professional Liability Early Warning Systems for Health Care Providers* (Chicago, Ill.: AHA, May 1986), 36.

17. American College of Obstetricians and Gynecologists, *Professional Liability and Its Effects*, 22.

18. Virginia Code, Section 38.2-5000-5021.

19. C. Gallup, "Can No-Fault Compensation of Impaired Infants Alleviate the Malpractice Crisis in Obstetrics?" *Journal of Health Politics, Policy and Law* 1989 14:691.

20. Florida Statutes, Section 60-75.

21. J. Holtzer, "Will No-Fault Insurance Work for Medical Malpractice?" *Resource Audio Digest* (March 1990).

SUGGESTED READINGS

Abraham, K.S. 1988. Medical liability reform: A conceptual framework. *Journal of the American Medical Association* 260:68.

American College of Obstetricians and Gynecologists, Committee on Ethics. October 1987. *Ethical issues related to expert testimony by obstetricians and gynecologists.* Washington, D.C.: ACOG.

Bedikian, M. 1984. Medical Malpractice Arbitration Act: Michigan's experience with arbitration. *American Journal of Law and Medicine* 10:287.

Botkin, J. 1988. The legal concept of wrongful life. *Journal of the American Medical Association* 259:1541–45.

Committee to Study Medical Professional Liability and the Delivery of Obstetrical Care, Institute of Medicine. 1989. *Medical Professional Liability and the Delivery of Obstetrical Care.* Washington, D.C.: National Academy Press.

Creighton, H. 1988. The nurse as an expert witness. *Nursing Management* 19:22.

Fiesta, J. 1983. *The law and liability: A guide for nurses.* New York: John Wiley & Sons.

Fineberg, K. et al. 1984. *Obstetrics/gynecology and the law.* Ann Arbor: Health Administration Press.

Harrington, L., M. Worth, Jr., and M. Carlucci. 1985. The development of the principles of medical malpractice in the United States. *Perspectives in Biology and Medicine* 29:41.

Heland, K., and P. Rutledge. 1988. Treatment: Tort reform and beyond. *Clinical Obstetrics and Gynecology* 31:209.

Holder, A. 1978. *Medical malpractice law.* 2nd ed. New York: John Wiley & Sons.

Johnson, K. et al. 1989. A fault-based administrative alternative for resolving medical malpractice claims. *Vanderbilt Law Review* 42:1365.

Lebow, M. 1988. America's schizophrenia: Public understanding of the malpractice question. *Clinical Obstetrics and Gynecology* 31:217.

Miller, F. 1986. Medical malpractice: Do the British have a better remedy? *American Journal of Law and Medicine* 11:433.

Miller, N. 1988. The standard of care in medical malpractice action. *For the Defense* 30 (December): 7.

Northrop, C., and M. Kelly. 1987. *Legal issues in nursing.* St. Louis: C.V. Mosby Co.

Perlis, D., and M. Brucker. 1983. Malpractice: A professional risk. *Journal of Nurse-Midwifery* 28 (March/April): 3.

Ramson, J. 1989. Nursing liability: Confusion in the courts. *For the Defense* 31 (March): 13.

Rosenblatt, R., and A. Hurst. 1989. An analysis of closed obstetric malpractice claims. *Obstetrics and Gynecology* 74:710.

Chapter 3

Abortion

3

Abortion is an often controversial topic and also quite unusual from a legal and risk management viewpoint. Most topics in this book are governed by state statutes with few directly relevant federal cases and statutes. In contrast, the legal background of abortion is largely federal in nature—based on constitutional grounds as refined by the U.S. Supreme Court. State statutes and regulations are limited to those permitted the states by federal law. Federal and state law are discussed in this chapter.

Although abortion is legal in the United States and has become the most commonly performed surgical procedure, there is no legal requirement that all health care providers or facilities provide abortion services. Those who choose to provide abortions still retain a great deal of power in deciding how and on whom the procedure is to be performed.

LEGAL STATUS OF ABORTION

Law in the United States before 1973

At common law in both England and America abortion, especially when it took place before quickening, was not a crime.[1] In fact, the literature shows that women sought abortion freely as a dependable form of birth control until the mid-nineteenth century.[2] The first English

51

abortion statute was enacted in 1803.[3] The first abortion statute in the United States appeared in Connecticut in 1821; it made abortion after quickening illegal.[4] In the United States, at least 31 states had statutes punishing the procurement of an abortion by a woman or someone on her behalf prior to the Civil War. Abortion legislation appeared to develop more quickly after the discovery of the ovum in 1827.[5] By 1900 abortion was illegal in all U.S. jurisdictions.[6] Liberalization of abortion law began in 1920 and accelerated after World War II.

A survey of state statutes in place in 1967 showed that Louisiana, Massachusetts, New Jersey, and Pennsylvania were the only states that had statutes prohibiting abortion without exception. Even in those states, there were court decisions permitting abortion at least where the life of the mother was endangered. In 44 other states and the District of Columbia, criminal statutes applicable to abortion permitted the procedure if it was necessary to save the life of the mother. These statutes variously classified criminal abortion as a felony or a misdemeanor. Punishment for the offense also varied. Several states increased the punishment if the pregnant woman died as a result of the abortion procedure, while in others it was possible to charge the abortionist with criminally negligent manslaughter or with second degree murder.[7]

In addition to criminal penalties applicable to the abortionist (penalties were not usually applicable to the woman seeking the abortion), most jurisdictions authorized revocation of a physician's license to practice medicine when he or she had performed or participated in an illegal abortion.[8] Statistics for 1965 show that 235 deaths, or 20 percent of all deaths related to pregnancy and childbirth in the United States, were attributable to illegal abortion.[9]

Between 1967 and 1972 there was a trend toward liberalizing state abortion laws.[10] Generally, these changes meant that abortion would be permitted when the health of the mother was considered in danger—a much broader standard than the one requiring proof that the mother's life was threatened.

Nevertheless, by 1969 an estimated 1 million criminal abortions were being performed each year in the United States. These abortions resulted in 250 to 300 maternal deaths per year and made illegal abortion the leading cause of maternal mortality during the years prior to 1973.[11]

Roe v. Wade and Its Progeny

The Supreme Court of the United States heard oral arguments in *Roe v. Wade* in December 1971. The Court requested and heard further argument during the next term and on January 22, 1973, issued its long-awaited opinion in the case.[12] The Court relied on the Fourteenth Amendment to the Constitution to find an inherent right to privacy protecting procreative choice. It held that the Constitution limits the powers of the states to restrict the availability of abortions. Generally, the pregnant woman, in consultation with her physician, has a constitutional right to decide to have an abortion. That right is to be balanced against two state interests: (1) the preservation of the woman's health during the abortion process and (2) potential human life.

In balancing a woman's rights and those of the state, the Court divided the pregnancy into three stages. During the first trimester, the "abortion decision . . . must be left to the medical judgment of the pregnant woman [and her] attending physician."[13] The states could adopt regulations if they were justified by important state health concerns, but these regulations could have "no significant impact" on the exercise of the woman's rights.[14] For example, the Court has permitted the state to require that special records be kept on abortions and that all tissue undergo pathology examination, even though it increased the cost of a first trimester abortion by 10 to 20 percent.[15]

During the second trimester or until viability (determined in a later case to be a medical judgment), the Court held that states could adopt regulations reasonably related to the mother's health. While *Roe v. Wade* suggested that a state could require that all second trimester abortions be performed in a hospital, a later case invalidated such an Ohio requirement.[16] In doing so, the Court relied on medical information that clinics were no less safe for patients than hospitals for the performance of second trimester abortions.

The Court held that after viability the state may, but need not, prohibit all abortions except those required to preserve maternal life or health.

Since *Roe v. Wade* the Court has decided abortion-related cases nearly every term. These cases review aspects of state laws that have developed in response to earlier Supreme Court decisions. There are also many other state and federal court decisions on various points.

ABORTION INCIDENCE AND MORTALITY

Many states have mandatory reporting systems for induced abortion that provide unique data for analysis. Some states require the use of a special reporting form, while others collect information on a fetal death report.[17] Cumulative statistics are then reported by the Centers for Disease Control (CDC).

In 1972 there were 586,760 legal abortions reported to the CDC; in 1981, there were 1.3 million.[18] Table 3-1 indicates the characteristics of women who had legal abortions in 1981 compared with those in 1972.

During 1981, seven women died after legal abortions (this figure excludes deaths from ectopic pregnancy), three after spontaneous abortions, and one after an illegal abortion, for a total of 11 deaths.[19] The CDC reported that the woman who died after an illegal abortion was 41 years old. She had not consulted a physician about her pregnancy nor had she sought a legal abortion. She died of a massive air embolism after she attempted to self-induce an abortion with a plastic straw.[20] In 1972, there were 90 abortion-related deaths known to the CDC. Of these, 39 resulted from illegally induced abortions.[21]

REIMBURSEMENT FOR ABORTION SERVICES

Beginning in 1976 various versions of the so-called Hyde Amendment severely limited the use of federal funds to reimburse states for the costs of abortion under the Medicaid program. In 1980 the Supreme Court, in *Harris v. McRae*,[22] upheld the constitutionality of this policy by stating that the government in "disbursing its Medicaid funds . . . is free to implement rationally what *Roe v. Wade* recognized to be its legitimate interest in a potential life by covering the medical costs of childbirth but denying funds for abortions."[23]

This decision did not prohibit states from funding abortions without federal reimbursement. Some state courts have found that failure to fund Medicaid abortions violates the relevant state constitution. Legislatures in other states have chosen to fund abortions for financially needy women.[24]

Table 3–1 Characteristics of Women Having Legal Abortions, 1972 and 1981

	1972	1981
Number of Legal Abortions	586,760	1,300,760
Residence		
Abortion in state	56.2%	92.5%
Abortion out of state	43.8	7.5
Age		
19 or younger	32.6%	28.0%
20–24	32.5	35.3
25 or older	34.9	36.7
Race		
White	77.0%	69.9%
Black and other	23.0	30.1
Marital Status		
Married	29.7%	22.1%
Unmarried	70.3	77.9
No. of Live Births		
Zero	49.4%	58.3%
One	18.2	19.7
Two	13.3	13.7
Three	8.7	5.3
Four or more	10.4	3.0
Type Procedure		
Curettage	88.6%	96.1%
Suction	65.2	90.4
Sharp	23.4	5.7
Intrauterine instillation	10.4	2.8
Hysterotomy/hysterectomy	0.6	0.1
Other	0.5	1.0
Weeks' Gestation		
Less than 8	34.0%	51.2%
9–10	30.7	26.8
11–12	17.5	12.1
13–15	8.4	5.2
16–20	8.2	3.7
Greater than 20 weeks	1.3	1.0

Source: Adapted from *Abortion Surveillance, Annual Summary 1981*, by U.S. Department of Health and Human Services, Public Health Service, Centers for Disease Control, p. iv, November 1985.

STATE REGULATION OF ABORTION SERVICES

States remain free to legislate or regulate aspects of abortion practice within U.S. Supreme Court guidelines. For example, some states have further defined the trimesters, and others prohibit abortion during the third trimester of pregnancy except where it is necessary to save the life or health of the mother. The states have been required to consider the following questions.

Who may perform abortions?

States uniformly require that abortions be performed by licensed physicians. Other individuals who perform abortions may be punished.

What records must be kept?

As noted above, the Supreme Court has agreed that states may require special records to be kept on abortion procedures. The states can require hospitals and clinics to report data on numbers and types of abortions, names of physicians, complications, and other statistical information. Some states do not require that patient names be reported; those that do usually state that such information will be kept confidential.

Where may the abortion be done?

Abortions may not be restricted to hospitals, at least during the first and second trimesters. States may set reasonable, medically justified standards for personnel, equipment, tissue examination, and counseling. These requirements may not unreasonably restrict patient access to abortion services. A state probably could require that an abortion after viability must be performed in a licensed hospital.

May spousal approval be required?

The Supreme Court has held that spousal approval may not be required prior to an abortion.[25] Several states continue to have spousal consent requirements on their statute books, but these statutes should be unenforceable.

May spousal notification prior to abortion be required?

Some states have written spousal notification requirements into statutes. The Supreme Court has not yet ruled directly on this point. Some commentators note that since spousal consent cannot be required prior to abortion, a notice provision may do nothing more than create a barrier to abortion. Others argue that such a requirement can promote family unity. Spousal notification depends on a patient's reliable reporting of her marital status. Generally, the health care provider has no legal obligation to require documentary evidence of marital status.

May a spouse or father of the conceptus prevent an abortion?

All courts that have addressed this issue have held that the father of the conceptus may not sue successfully to prevent a legal abortion.

May a parent, boyfriend, or spouse force a pregnant woman to have an abortion?

Again, courts have held that a woman, even a minor, may not be compelled to undergo an unwanted abortion.[26] The father of the baby may not compel a woman to abort, even though he will remain liable for child support payments for his unwanted child.

Who can be billed for abortion services?

Abortions at any gestational age are not inexpensive, although first trimester abortions cost less than abortions performed later. Many abortion services have sliding fees for patients who are financially less able. Because abortion facilities do not care to bill patients (or their parents), it has become customary to require cash payment at or before the time of an outpatient abortion. While in theory parents remain financially responsible for their minor child's necessary medical expenses, most health care providers and abortion facilities do not wish to notify parents, by making an attempt to collect payment, that an abortion has been done without parental consent.

PATIENT CONSENT

Therapeutic or medically indicated abortions may be done only after the patient's consent (or, in rare instances, the consent of a guardian) has been obtained. States or hospitals may require that the consent be reduced to writing. Information about the abortion procedure, including its costs, risks, benefits, and failure rates, should be provided. Some states require presentation of information about alternatives to abortion. The U.S. Supreme Court has invalidated state statutory language requiring that the patient be told of fetal development and characteristics present at the time of the abortion.[27] This decision probably also renders unconstitutional statutes that, for example, require a physician to tell the woman about analgesia for fetal pain.

In general, it is advisable for a physician who performs an abortion to verify the patient's consent to the procedure if that physician has not participated in the entire discussion. The U.S. Supreme Court has held, however, that while a physician remains responsible for the medical aspects of the abortion, the state cannot require that all information be communicated by the physician personally.[28] The state may require, however, that counseling be done by those "qualified" to do it. Prescribed waiting periods between the signing of the consent form and the abortion are not permitted,[29] except perhaps where a statute requires it for a minor.[30]

State Laws Regarding Minors

The law concerning consent to abortion services by minors is rather complex. In the absence of a statute, a minor who is capable of consenting may do so without parental or judicial consent. When a minor is unemancipated and her ability to understand and provide an informed consent seems questionable, the U.S. Supreme Court has held that the state may require parental or judicial consent.[31] If the state requires parental consent under certain circumstances, the statute must provide for an anonymous, expeditious judicial review in the event the minor declines to obtain parental consent.[32] Several states have provided procedures of this type. In general, the judge may certify only that the minor is or is not capable of consenting or that the abortion is in the minor's best interests.[33]

A Massachusetts law provides an example of this type of statute. It was first passed in 1974 and was judged unconstitutional in *Bellotti v. Baird*[34] in 1979. The law was revised in 1980 and became effective in 1981. It requires an unmarried woman under 18 years of age to obtain the notarized, in-person consent of *both* parents, or of a superior court judge, before an abortion can be done. If judicial consent is sought, the judge must find that the minor is mature enough to consent or that the abortion is in her best interests. A study of the effect of this law was published in 1986. The study showed that after the implementation of the law about one-third of all Massachusetts resident minors who obtained abortions did so in nearby, less restrictive states. Of those minors who obtained abortions within Massachusetts, 75 percent had parental consent. The rest sought judicial consent. The study found that the law had no impact on the number of teenage pregnancies in Massachusetts.[35]

In states with laws requiring consent of both parents, it may be necessary for a custodial parent and the child to go to court to have the consent requirement for the other parent waived. This is true in Minnesota where the statute requires notice to the other parent even if the parents are living apart or divorced.[36]

A number of states now have laws requiring parental notification prior to an abortion. Supreme Court decisions and state laws are still evolving on this point, but it appears that an adequately drafted statute may be constitutional.

ABORTION MEDICAL RECORDS

The medical records of adults are to be kept confidential under the laws of most states and by common law. A problem may arise with minors. Typically, for example, the parents of minors may request and receive medical records from a hospital. These records could include records from a previously unknown abortion. The minor may try to avoid this problem by obtaining an abortion at a facility apart from her usual source of medical care. Further, some state statutes allow a health care facility to refuse to release medical records, regardless of the age of the patient, if that release may be harmful to the patient.

INSTITUTIONAL POLICIES

The U.S. Supreme Court and state court decisions have addressed the powers of government to regulate abortions. Physicians, clinics, and hospitals, however, may make their own rules, some or all of which may be more restrictive than courts would allow a state to make. For example, a hospital may decide that no elective abortions will be done on its premises or that only first trimester abortions will be done. A physician may decide to perform abortions on minors only with parental consent. A hospital may permit a first trimester abortion on a minor without parental consent but refuse to allow a second trimester abortion on the same patient, perhaps because hospitalization may be required or because of increased risk or reimbursement requirements.

ABORTION SERVICES

Subject to the many rules and regulations discussed above and subject to professional liability fears, abortion services are delivered in all states.

During the first trimester, most abortions are done by suction curettage. The more common complications of first trimester abortions include endometritis (0.75 percent), excessive bleeding and retained products of conception (0.61 percent).[37] Patients should be informed of these risks prior to the procedure and should be given discharge instructions, since these complications may be manifested days or weeks after the procedure itself.

The risk of cervical injury is often considered less common, but an analysis of 15,438 suction abortions at 12 weeks' gestational age or less showed an incidence of 1.03 per 100 abortions.[38] The use of laminaria rather than rigid dilation decreased the incidence. The analysis revealed that the incidence of cervical injury was increased when abortions were done by residents rather than by attending physicians and when general anesthesia rather than local anesthesia was used. The risk was lower for women who had had one or more prior abortions.[39]

Another serious complication is uterine perforation. The incidence in one study of 67,175 curettage abortions done at 24 weeks' gestation or less was 0.9 per 1,000 abortions. The risk was higher with gestational age and when the abortion was performed by a resident rather than an attending physician.[40]

Because both cervical injury and uterine perforation can require admission to a hospital, at least for observation and possibly for surgery, prospective abortion patients should be warned of these risks. In particular, minors undergoing abortions without parental consent should be aware that their parents will be notified if hospital admission is needed.

Approximately 90 percent of all legal abortions in the United States in 1981 were performed during the first trimester.[41] Complications of first trimester abortions can include hemorrhage, trauma to the cervix (lacerations and fistula formation), infection, and retained products of conception. It has been estimated that mortality from induced abortion during the first 15 weeks of pregnancy is one-seventh the risk of dying from pregnancy and childbirth.[42] Up to about 16 weeks, dilation and evacuation (D&E) is said to be a feasible and safe procedure.[43]

Complication rates increase when the abortion must be accomplished by the injection of materials into the uterus for the induction of premature labor. Complications depend upon the type of substance injected, but they can include retained placenta (up to 50 percent of the cases), cervical injury, uterine rupture, and disseminated intravascular coagulation. Labor may not begin for 12 to 36 hours after injection.[44] This type of procedure is ordinarily performed within a licensed health care facility, usually a hospital or clinic, since laboratory, medical, and surgical services may be required.

Complexity and complication rates of second and third trimester abortions confirm the desirability of first trimester procedures when abortion is desired by the patient.

Professional Liability

A 1987 survey conducted by the American College of Obstetricians and Gynecologists showed that of the 1,449 gynecologic claims reported by 1,984 respondents to the survey, 99 (6.8 percent) of them had claims that were primarily abortion-related.[45] While the study does not show what was paid in those claims, the median gynecologic payment was $15,000 in the 497 claims that had been resolved.[46]

Professional liability allegations involving therapeutic abortion are often relatively minor. They may relate to missed abortion (failure to complete the abortion or retained products of conception) or endometritis. These and similar complications can and do occur in the absence of negligence on the part of the health care provider.

Other complications can result in more serious and thus potentially more costly claims. As an example, a maternal death from ectopic pregnancy following a failure to communicate tissue results consisting of decidua only is a tragic and expensive case.

In *Speck v. Finegold* (a case further discussed in Chapter 6), a Pennsylvania appeals court considered the following facts in the context of a wrongful life case. Mr. Speck and his two children suffered from neurofibromatosis. Mr. and Mrs. Speck decided to limit the size of their family, because they feared that additional children also would be afflicted. Mr. Speck underwent a vasectomy and was assured by the urologist that he and his wife could have intercourse without contraception. Mrs. Speck later became pregnant. She then underwent an abortion and was told it was successful. Some time after the abortion, Mrs. Speck informed the gynecologist that she felt like she was still pregnant, but the physician assured her that the pregnancy had been aborted. The patient later delivered a daughter afflicted with neurofibromatosis. The court held that the parents, if they could prove their allegations, could recover pecuniary damages for the expenses that they had borne, and would bear, for the care and treatment of their youngest daughter.[47]

Risk Management

The subject of risk management can be conveniently divided into three general areas: (1) the mechanics of an abortion service, including equipment and staffing; (2) direct patient contact; and (3) follow-up of patients and the performance of the clinical services. Each of these areas will be influenced to some extent by state and federal law (discussed above).

Organization of the Clinic

Both state regulatory and risk management concerns dictate that considerable attention be paid to the staff, equipment, and services provided by an abortion facility. Staff members should be hired on the basis of their qualifications to undertake their tasks in the provision of abortion services. They should receive sufficient orientation so that supervisory personnel can feel confident that tasks are being carried out competently. These principles also apply to the physician staff. New physicians should be supervised at least initially by physicians more experienced in doing abortions. This is particularly important, because studies show increased complication rates when the procedures are performed by less experienced personnel.

While some abortion facilities are freestanding, many others are organized as part of a larger facility such as a licensed hospital. In the latter case, administrative personnel should be aware of any state or institutional policies that allow personnel with a moral or religious objection to abortion to decline to provide abortion services. Administrative personnel should be quite clear about exact job requirements when interviewing both internal and external applicants for positions. This permits unsuitable employees to withdraw or be disqualified for consideration.

Adequate space, teaching aids, and personnel should be provided for the counseling portion of the abortion procedure. Since patients will require at least some laboratory screening (such as a determination of Rh factor) prior to the procedure, arrangements must be made between the facility and an appropriate laboratory. A reliable source for RhoGAM must be found, a laboratory for tissue examination be available, and ambulance arrangements made for emergencies. State regulations may also set facility standards through fire and building codes.

Patient Services

The clinic administration must determine what services will be offered. For example, will contraceptive services be provided the abortion patient? Will postabortion checks be done? How will referrals for cases inappropriate for the clinic be undertaken and to whom will the referrals be made?

When the services are determined, appropriate personnel and equipment can be procured. Policies must be determined for at least the following:

- patient medical eligibility/ineligibility
- appropriate gestational ages and the confirmation of gestational age where viability is approached
- contents of medical records, forms, and logbooks for patients and laboratory specimens
- fees and collections
- contents of counseling sessions
- appointment making
- preabortion procedures at the site
  - laboratory work
  - pregnancy testing
- postabortion contraceptive counseling
- consent procedures and forms
- abortion procedures
  - employee functions
  - equipment/sterilization
  - infection control procedures for blood and body fluids
  - analgesia/anesthesia
  - pathology
  - emergencies/contents of emergency box
- emergency transfer procedures
- postabortion recovery procedures and length of stay
- discharge instructions and adequate follow-up

The physician always must be permitted to refuse to perform abortions on inappropriate patients. These may include patients, for example, who are too many weeks into pregnancy, who have other medical problems that cannot be handled within the setting, or who cannot be relied upon to remain fairly still during an outpatient abortion under local anesthesia.

Written consent forms are used quite routinely for abortion services. There are many possible forms, from the very brief to the most detailed. The language in any type of form should be simple enough for most people to understand. If patients do not speak English adequately, translations of the form or translators should be available. The form can be read aloud and discussed with illiterate patients.

The form should include some information about the risks and benefits of the procedure and either a statement that these factors have been discussed with the patient or a list of topics that have been discussed. The patient should sign the form. Some facilities require that the patient's signature be witnessed. This requirement can serve a second function of noting the staff member who counseled the patient and answered her questions.

Some patients choose to use false names when they go to an abortion facility. Patients should be discouraged from doing this or providing a false address or telephone number. Instead, patients who are worried about release of abortion information should be told of clinic policies to maintain confidentiality. The critical importance of being able to contact the patient if, for example, the pathology on the abortion specimen contains no villi, should be emphasized.

Patient Follow-Up

All patients should be given adequate discharge instructions. An information sheet may be given to each patient, but it should not be substituted for verbal instructions. Any instructions should include information about bleeding, pain, fever, resumption of sexual activity, and the need for a postabortion check at two to three weeks postabortion. The postabortion examination could take place at the abortion facility or could be done at another site, but its importance needs emphasis.

The abortion facility must have an adequate system to ensure that all laboratory and pathology specimens have been returned and reviewed for abnormalities by the staff. When abnormalities are discovered, the patient must be contacted promptly and necessary follow-up arranged.

Medical records should also indicate missed appointments, the date and content of follow-up telephone calls that were made, and any correspondence with the patient. If the patient cannot be contacted by telephone about a laboratory report, it may be necessary to send a registered letter. This method should be used cautiously if the patient lives with others. The letter should be marked confidential and the return address should not refer to an abortion clinic. A copy of the letter should be filed in the patient's medical record. This kind of documentation can be useful in showing staff efforts to contact the patient about an important clinical matter.

Sexual Abuse Reporting Requirements

A patient may indicate to staff members that she has become pregnant as a result of sexual abuse or sexual assault. If a health care provider has reason to suspect sexual abuse, it should be reported to appropriate state authorities. A patient who complains of sexual assault should be assisted in making a report to the police.

PATIENT CASE

The following case of a legal abortion death, published by the CDC and called preventable, illustrates some of the problems that even the most carefully designed and operated abortion facility may encounter.

A 22-year-old black, unmarried, 11th grade student, gravida 1, with no pre-existing medical condition, underwent suction curettage plus sharp curettage in a physician's office for an estimated 12-week pregnancy. Payment was by private sources. Local anesthesia was given by paracervical block.

The young woman became uncooperative during the procedure and was given 5 mg diazepam intravenously. She remained uncooperative and, as a result, the procedure was halted. The physician recommended that the procedure be completed at a hospital. The patient, after discussing this recommendation with her mother, refused hospitalization. She felt she could cooperate sufficiently to allow completion of the procedure in the physician's office. Another 5 mg diazepam was given intravenously. However, soon after the procedure was resumed, the young woman "began to buck and have severe gyrating movement." The physician felt that, though he had evacuated the uterus thoroughly, he had perforated the anterior wall of the uterus. He again recommended hospitalization, which the patient again refused.

The patient was observed for three hours in the office, during which time she received intravenous oxytocin. Her vital signs remained stable; there was very little vaginal bleeding. Her hematocrit was 31 percent. The mother and daughter left the office after agreeing to return the following day. The physician called the home twice and was told that the patient was resting comfortably and bleeding minimally. The patient did not return to the office the next day as scheduled, but her mother called and told the doctor that her daughter was comfortable, resting well, feeling fine, and would return to the office the following day. However, that appointment also was not kept. The physician called the patient's home frequently to inquire about her condition, but was asked not to call anymore.

The family next contacted the physician 36 hours later (four days after the procedure) at 4 A.M. The mother, concerned that the patient was "not looking well," requested a house call. The physician responded and arrived at approximately 5 A.M. to find the young woman quite lethargic, but sitting upright and responsive. Emergency medical services were called; however, the young woman became unresponsive en route to the hospital. She was pronounced dead in the emergency room upon arrival. Her hematocrit was 18.4 percent; her hemoglobin was 5.6 gm/dl. Death was attributed to uterine perforation, intra-abdominal hemorrhage, and peritonitis. No autopsy was performed.[48]

The CDC suggests that the gestation of this pregnancy may have exceeded 12 weeks and that the abortion could more safely have been performed in a facility other than an office. It notes that the patient's behavior in failing to use contraception to prevent an unwanted pregnancy and in failing to accept later recommended treatment and follow-up were major factors contributing to her death.

The CDC report does not state whether a professional liability action was brought after this maternal death. Such an action could have been defended, particularly if the physician had carefully documented his care, advice, and telephone calls and patient response.

THE FUTURE OF ABORTION SERVICES

Opponents of abortion continue to press the U.S. Supreme Court and government officials to make most or all abortions illegal. Nearly every term the Supreme Court considers a case that may provide an opportunity for reconsideration of its *Roe v. Wade* decision. Should that case be overruled, abortions would not become illegal. Instead, state legislatures again would be permitted to make individual rules for abortion services in their states.

The Supreme Court decided *Webster v. Reproductive Health Services* on July 3, 1989. The case concerned a Missouri law, found unconstitutional by two lower federal courts, that among other things had banned the performance of abortions in publicly supported facilities in the state. In a long anticipated opinion, the Court retreated from what Justice Rehnquist called the "rigid trimester system" used in *Roe* and allowed the states more regulatory power. On the specific aspects of the Missouri law, the Court found that a state could declare that life begins at conception in the preamble to the statute (but could not use the declaration as a basis for limiting abortion rights), could ban the performance of abortions in public facilities and by public employees unless the pregnancy was life-threatening, and could require physicians to perform testing to determine potential viability if the abortion is to be done after 20 weeks.[49]

Earlier law decided using the *Roe* decision remains undisturbed for the time being. However, the Court is scheduled to hear two more cases during the 1989–1990 term. Both concern abortion rights for minors. These decisions will be an important signal about how far the Court intends to permit states to regulate abortion rights. Meanwhile, some state legislatures may act to restrict abortion rights by statute. Some of these laws may be found unconstitutional by state courts. But if not, and if appealed, these laws will provide the U.S. Supreme Court with further opportunity to examine abortion law.

NOTES

1. K. Niswander and M. Porto, "Abortion Practices in the United States: A Medical Viewpoint," in *Abortion, Medicine and the Law*, eds. J.D. Butler and D. Walbert (New York: Facts on File Publications, 1986), 249.

2. J. Raisler, "Abortion 1980: Battleground for Reproductive Rights," *Journal of Nurse-Midwifery* 25 (March/April 1980):28.

3. H. David, "Abortion Policies," in *Abortion and Sterilization: Medical and Social Aspects*, ed. J. Hodgson (New York: Grune & Stratton, 1981), 5.

4. Ibid.

5. W. Marshner, "Statement," in *Abortion, Medicine and the Law*, 647.

6. David, "Abortion Policies," 7.

7. B.J. George, Jr., "The Evolving Law of Abortion," *Case Western Reserve Law Review* 23 (1972): 715–20.

8. Ibid., 727.

9. Niswander and Porto, "Abortion Practices," 248.

10. Ibid., 708.

11. Raisler, "Abortion 1980", 29.

12. *Roe v. Wade*, 410 U.S. 113 (1973).

13. Ibid., 164.

14. *Akron v. Akron Center for Reproductive Health*, 462 U.S. 416 (1983), 430.

15. *Planned Parenthood Association of Kansas City v. Ashcroft*, 462 U.S. 476, 486–90.

16. *Akron v. Akron Center for Reproductive Health*, 462 U.S. 416 (1983), 431–39.

17. U.S. Public Health Service, National Center for Health Statistics, *Handbook on the Reporting of Induced Termination of Pregnancy* [U.S. Government pamphlet] (Hyattsville, Md., January 1986), 2.

18. U.S. Public Health Service, Centers for Disease Control, *Abortion Surveillance: Annual Summary 1981* [U.S. Government pamphlet] (November 1985), iv (Summary Table).

19. Ibid., 1.

20. Ibid., 12.

21. Ibid., 51.

22. *Harris v. McRae*, 448 U.S. 297 (1980).

23. Ibid., 48 U.S. Law Week 4949.

24. W. Cates, Jr. "The Hyde Amendment in Action," *Journal of the American Medical Association* 246 (1981): 1109.

25. *Planned Parenthood of Central Missouri v. Danforth*, 428 U.S. 52.

26. See *In re Smith*, 295 A.2d 238 (Md. 1972); *In the Matter of Mary P*, 444 N.Y.S.2d 545 (N.Y. 1981).

27. *Akron v. Akron Center for Reproductive Health*, 462 U.S. 416 (1983).

28. *Akron v. Akron Center for Reproductive Health*, 462 U.S. 416 (1983), 446–49.

29. Ibid.

30. See *Hodgson v. State of Minnesota*, 853 F.2d 1452 (8th Cir. 1988).

31. See J. Benshoof and H. Pilpel, "Minors' Rights to Confidential Abortions: The Evolving Legal Scene," in *Abortion, Medicine and the Law*, eds. J.D. Butler and D. Walbert (New York: Facts on File Publications, 1986), 137–60.

32. *Bellotti v. Baird*, 433 U.S. 622 (1979).

33. However, in contrast, see *Matter of Moe*, 532 N.E.2d 794 (Mass. App. Ct. 1988).

34. *Bellotti v. Baird*, 433 U.S. 622 (1979).

35. V. Cartoof and L. Klerman, "Parental Consent for Abortion: Impact of the Massachusetts Law," *American Journal of Public Health* 76 (April 1986): 397.

36. Minn. Stat. Section 144. 343 (2–4).

37. Niswander and Porto, "Abortion Practices," 259.

38. U.S. Public Health Service, *Abortion Surveillance*, 14.

39. Ibid.

40. Ibid., 15.

41. U.S. Public Health Service, *Abortion Surveillance*, iv.

42. S. LeBolt, et al., "Mortality from Abortion and Childbirth: Are the Populations Comparable?", *Journal of the American Medical Association* 248 (1983): 188.

43. A. Guttmacher and I. Kaiser, "The Genesis of Liberalized Abortion in New York: A Personal Insight," in *Abortion, Medicine and the Law*, eds. J.D. Butler and D. Walbert (New York: Facts on File Publications, 1986), 243.

44. Ibid., 243–44.

45. American College of Obstetricians and Gynecologists, *Professional Liability and Its Effects: Report of a 1987 Survey of ACOG's Membership* (Washington, D.C.: ACOG, March 1988), Table 23.

46. Ibid., Table 35.

47. *Speck v. Finegold*, 408 A.2d 496 (Pa. 1979).

48. Adapted from U.S. Public Health Service, *Abortion Surveillance*, 11–12.

49. *Webster v. Reproductive Health Services*, 109 S. Ct. 3040 (1989).

SUGGESTED READINGS

Annas, G. 1989. The Supreme Court, privacy, and abortion. *New England Journal of Medicine* 321 (October 26): 1200.

Atrash, H. et al. 1987. Legal abortion mortality in the United States: 1972–1982. *American Journal of Obstetrics and Gynecology* 156: 605.

Baron, C. 1989. Abortion and the legal process in the United States: An overview of the post-Webster legal landscape. *Law, Medicine and Healthcare* 17:368.

Cates, W., Jr. et al. 1982. Mortality from abortion and childbirth: Are the statistics biased? *Journal of the American Medical Association* 248: 192.

Donovan, P. 1983. Judging teenagers: How minors fare when they seek court-authorized abortions. *Family Planning Perspectives* 15: 259.

Holder, A. 1985. *Legal issues in pediatrics and adolescent medicine*. 2nd ed. New Haven, Conn.: Yale University Press.

Isaacs, S., and R. Cook. 1984. Laws and policies affecting fertility: A decade of change. *Population Reports* 12 (November): E105.

Mahowald, M., and V. Abernethy. 1985. Case study: When a mentally ill woman refuses abortion. *Hastings Center Report* (April): 22–24.

Planned Parenthood League of Connecticut. 1987. *Let's tell the truth about abortion.* New Haven, Conn.: PPLC.

Planned Parenthood League of Massachusetts. 1986. *Questions and answers about abortion: A handbook for citizens of Massachusetts.* Cambridge, Mass.: PPLC.

Sollom, T., and P. Donovan. 1985. State laws and the provision of family planning and abortion services in 1985. *Family Planning Perspectives* 17 (November/December): 262.

Tietze, C., and S. Henshaw. 1986. *Induced abortion: A world review, 1986.* 6th ed. Washington, D.C.: The Alan Guttmacher Institute.

Chapter 4

Sterilization

It has been estimated that more than 100 million people worldwide have been sterilized.[1] By 1982 sterilization had become the most popular method of contraception among married women in the United States.[2] During 1984, the last year for which statistics are available, more than 730,000 female sterilization procedures were performed, compared with 418,500 vasectomies.[3]

Fortunately, female tubal sterilization is a relatively safe procedure. Most studies estimate the death rate attributable to the surgery as 2 to 3 per 100,000 procedures.[4] Deaths are usually related to anesthesia, infection, or hemorrhage. Most complications are minor, such as superficial wound infections, but major complications can include bowel perforation, vessel lacerations causing major hemorrhage, and tetanus. Early recognition and prompt treatment of complications contribute to the low mortality rate.

DEVELOPMENT OF THE LAW

Voluntary sterilization is legal for a majority of the world's population.[5] In the United States and other countries with common law systems, sterilization generally is legal because no law prohibits it. Current law in this country restricts sterilization under certain circumstances, because abuses have occurred in the past. There was an influential political movement during the 1890s that advocated eugenic sterilization, and new procedures, such as vasectomy and salpingectomy, were developed to replace castration. These developments contributed to the passage in Indiana of the first eugenic sterilization act in 1907.[6] This law provided for sterilization of inmates of state mental hospitals and prisons and residents of homes for the "feeble-minded." Individuals who were judged insane, idiotic, moronic, or imbecilic could be sterilized. By the 1930s, more than 30 states had passed similar laws, often with an expanded list of so-called hereditary defects, including alcoholism and drug addiction, as well as blindness and deafness.[7] Many laws were challenged and rarely enforced in some states, but other states had active eugenic sterilization programs. Between 1907 and 1963, more than 60,000 people were sterilized pursuant to eugenic sterilization programs in 30 states.[8]

The Supreme Court, in *Buck v. Bell*,[9] upheld a Virginia sterilization law in 1927. The law provided that a superintendent of a state institution, such as the Virginia Colony for Epileptics and the Feeble-Minded, could have an inmate sterilized if it was the superintendent's opinion that the surgery was in the best interests of the patient and of society. Certain procedural safeguards for the patient were provided in the law, including notice, the appointment of a guardian for the patient (if one had not already been appointed), and a hearing with rights of appeal. In famous language, Justice Oliver Wendell Holmes wrote, in part, that "[i]t is better for all the world, if instead of waiting to execute degenerate offspring for crime, or to let them starve for their imbecility, society can prevent those who are manifestly unfit from continuing their kind. The principle that sustains compulsory vaccination is broad enough to cover cutting the Fallopian tubes. Three generations of imbeciles are enough."[10]

In 1942 the Supreme Court retreated from the *Buck v. Bell* decision when it held in *Skinner v. Oklahoma*[11] that the state's Habitual Criminal Sterilization Act was unconstitutional. Under that law, a habitual criminal was defined as one who had been convicted two or more times for crimes "amounting to felonies involving moral turpitude" in any state and who was then convicted of such a felony in Oklahoma and sentenced to jail. In *Skinner* the law was to be applied to a man who had been convicted of stealing chickens in 1926, of armed robbery in 1929, and then of another armed robbery. The statute was struck down, not because involuntary sterilization was considered improper, but because the law exempted certain white-collar criminals and thus did not treat all habitual offenders equally.

Since then many states have repealed eugenic sterilization statutes; however, 19 states still had laws in 1985 that permitted the eugenic sterilization of institutionalized retarded persons.[12] Such laws are now rarely used and are subject to constitutional challenge.[13]

While sterilization procedures may be legal, private hospitals may enforce rules to prohibit elective or nonemergency sterilizations. A hospital owned by a religious order, for example, could prohibit scheduled elective tubal ligations but probably could not discipline a physician who performs emergency surgery in which sterilization is an unavoidable byproduct. Courts have held that a publicly owned hospital may not prohibit consensual sterilization.[14]

CURRENT LAW

Consent to Sterilization

A majority of states do not explicitly regulate sterilization procedures. Those that do confirm that a competent adult may consent to sterilization. Connecticut and certain other states prohibit the sterilization of anyone under the age of 18.[15] Where state law does not prohibit the sterilization of minors, considerable caution should precede sterilization surgery. In most states minors who have borne children are thereby emancipated, but this is not universally true. Parental consent would be required for sterilization of a minor who is not emancipated, but this requirement should not be considered dispositive, especially if the minor objects to the surgery. Emancipation by itself should not delude a physician into believing that the minor is capable of the judgment that an adult may have. Requests for sterilization of minors should be examined individually, and considerable care should go into consent discussions and their documentation.

Spousal consent to sterilization is not required in the United States[16] and in most western nations. It is not unusual for patients who have never borne children to request sterilization. The law does not prohibit these procedures, but the physician should take the time to ensure that the patient fully understands the implications of the request. As with other surgical procedures, an individual physician may decline a request for elective sterilization surgery if he or she believes it to be unwise or unsafe or it is in violation of the physician's personal beliefs.

When the patient is unable to give consent (for example, if the patient is retarded or mentally disabled), two solutions have evolved by statute. (Exhibit 4-1 lists those states with statutes regulating sterilization of the mentally incompetent.) Some states provide that a patient who has been denied the opportunity to consent, the patient's parents or guardians, or state custodians may petition a state court for permission to sterilize. After the petition is filed, the court appoints a lawyer to represent the prospective patient and hears evidence from those who have examined the patient.[17] Generally, the court will permit another person to give consent for sterilization only if it finds that the surgery is in the best interests of the patient. Statutes in other states prohibit the sterilization of an individual who is unable to consent to the procedure.

The majority of states have no statutes addressing consent when the patient is incompetent. While courts often refuse to permit sterilization, even when faced with a good-faith request from a caring family,[18] some courts have agreed to decide even in the absence of a statute. For example, the Massachusetts Supreme Court has held that in the absence of enabling legislation, the probate court has jurisdiction to act on a request for sterilization of an incompetent person.[19] The decision set forth the same types of protections often found in the statutes on this

Exhibit 4–1   States with Statutes Regulating Sterilization of the Mentally Incompetent

Alabama	Oklahoma
Arkansas	Oregon
Connecticut	South Carolina
Delaware	Texas
Georgia	Utah
Idaho	Vermont
Maine	Virginia
Mississippi	Washington
North Carolina	Wisconsin
North Dakota	

point. There must be notice, a hearing, a guardian ad litem for the patient, and the appointment, if necessary, of independent medical and psychological experts to examine the patient. The following facts should enter into the decision-making process:

- physical ability of the incompetent person to procreate
- a finding that other means of contraception are not feasible (with the sterilization procedure being the least intrusive alternative)
- medical need, if any, for the procedure
- nature and extent of the person's disability (taking into account the capacity of the individual to care for a child with assistance and the possibility that the person might marry and have the assistance of a spouse in child care)
- a probability that the person will engage in sexual activity resulting in pregnancy
- likelihood of health risks, including trauma and psychological harm from sterilization, pregnancy, or childbirth[20]

Some commentators also believe that the incompetent patient must be represented by counsel during the proceedings.

These cases are often quite complicated, and court preparation (including court-mandated examinations) can be time-consuming. The outcome is not certain, since the court must decide what the incompetent person would have wanted, instead of merely doing what family members may find convenient or desirable. The process also may be expensive for the person petitioning the court. Less cumbersome procedures are unlikely to evolve, because courts have held that procreation is a protected right. The permanent removal of that right by sterilization requires legal protection to prevent the types of abuses that occurred earlier in this century.

Content of Consent

Sterilization is a surgical procedure. Written consent is advisable and may be necessary under state law. Most authorities recommend that the following information be part of a discussion with the patient prior to the patient signing a consent form:

- alternatives to sterilization
- risks of the procedure (specific to the type recommended), including short- and long-term complications
- failure rates (studies indicate some variation but a failure rate of 4 per 1,000 procedures can be expected)[21]
- permanence (the surgery must be considered permanent—tubes usually cannot be "untied"), but with no guarantee to the patient of the procedure's success
- description of the procedure, including costs and prospective recovery period

Some surgeons and facilities use consent forms that discuss much of this information in detail; others have chosen a simpler form. When a detailed form is used, it should be available in languages other than English as needed. The form should use wording that most people can read and understand. An informed person must be available to answer questions. If the population served is, or may be, functionally illiterate, a detailed form may not be practical. The patient should sign the consent form, but a witnessed mark or "X" is acceptable if the patient cannot write.

If payment is to be made from federal funds (and, in some places, state funds as well), there are applicable federal regulations to prevent sterilization abuse of poor women.[22] A consent form specific to federally funded procedures is required by these regulations (see Exhibit 4–2).

The form must be signed at least 30 days prior to the procedure (but within 180 days). If the patient delivers prematurely or has emergency abdominal surgery during which sterilization is performed, the physician must certify that the form has been signed at least 72 hours prior to the delivery or surgery.[23] Federal funding will not pay for sterilization procedures on women under 21 years of age. This restriction is unaffected by state laws making 18 years the age of majority or by any other law. It has undergone constitutional challenge by women with children under age 21, and it has been upheld.[24]

Exhibit 4-2 Sample Consent Form for Sterilization

CONSENT FORM

NOTICE: YOUR DECISION AT ANY TIME NOT TO BE STERILIZED WILL NOT RESULT IN THE WITHDRAWAL OR WITHHOLDING OF ANY BENEFITS PROVIDED BY PROGRAMS OR PROJECTS RECEIVING FEDERAL FUNDS.

CONSENT TO STERILIZATION

I have asked for and received information about sterilization from _____ _____. When I first asked for the information, I was told that the
(doctor or clinic)
decision to be sterilized is completely up to me. I was told that I could decide not to be sterilized. If I decide not to be sterilized, my decision will not affect my right to future care or treatment. I will not lose any help or benefits from programs receiving federal funds, such as AFDC or Medicaid that I am now getting or for which I may become eligible.

I UNDERSTAND THAT THE STERILIZATION MUST BE CONSIDERED PERMANENT AND NOT REVERSIBLE. I HAVE DECIDED THAT I DO NOT WANT TO BECOME PREGNANT, BEAR CHILDREN, OR FATHER CHILDREN.

I was told about those temporary methods of birth control that are available and could be provided to me which will allow me to bear or father a child in the future. I have rejected these alternatives and chosen to be sterilized.

I understand that I will be sterilized by an operation known as a _____ _____. The discomforts, risks, and benefits associated with the operation have been explained to me. All my questions have been answered to my satisfaction.

I understand that the operation will not be done until at least 30 days after I sign this form. I understand that I can change my mind at any time and that my decision at any time not to be sterilized will not result in the withholding of any benefits or medical services provided by federally funded programs.

I am at least 21 years of age and was born on _____.
                                                                                                              Month   Day   Year

I, _____, hereby consent of my own free will to be sterilized by _____ by a method called _____.
              (doctor)

My consent expires 180 days from the date of my signature below.

I also consent to the release of this form and other medical records about the operation to:

Representatives of the Department of Health and Human Services or

Employees of programs or projects funded by that department but only for determining if federal laws were observed.

I have received a copy of this form.

_____ Date:_____
Signature   *Month   Day   Year*

You are requested to supply the following information, but it is not required:
Race and ethnicity designation (please check)

Exhibit 4–2   continued

__American Indian or   __Black (not of Hispanic origin)
    Alaska Native   __Hispanic
__Asian or Pacific Islander   __White (not of Hispanic origin)

INTERPRETER'S STATEMENT

If an interpreter is provided to assist the individual to be sterilized:
I have translated the information and advice presented orally to the individual to be sterilized by the person obtaining this consent. I have also read him/her the consent form in _____ language and explained its contents to him/her. To the best of my knowledge and belief he/she understood this explanation.

_____   _____
Interpreter   *Date*

STATEMENT OF PERSON OBTAINING CONSENT

Before _____ signed the consent form, I
                    (name of individual)
explained to him/her the nature of the sterilization operation _____;
the fact that it is intended to be a final and irreversible procedure; and the discomforts, risks, and benefits associated with it.

I counseled the individual to be sterilized that alternative methods of birth control are available which are temporary. I explained that sterilization is different because it is permanent.

I informed the individual to be sterilized that his/her consent can be withdrawn at any time and that he/she will not lose any health services or any benefits provided by federal funds.

To the best of my knowledge and belief the individual to be sterilized is at least 21 years old and appears mentally competent. He/she knowingly and voluntarily requested to be sterilized and appears to understand the nature and consequences of the procedure.

_____   _____
Signature of person obtaining consent   *Date*

_____
Facility

_____
Address

PHYSICIAN'S STATEMENT

Shortly before I performed a sterilization operation upon _____
                                                (name of individual to be

_____on _____, I explained to him/her
sterilized)   *(date of sterilization operation)*
the nature of the sterilization operation _____; the fact
                                        (specify type of operation)
that it is intended to be a final and irreversible procedure; and the discomforts, risks, and benefits associated with it.

Exhibit 4–2 continued

> I counseled the individual to be sterilized that alternative methods of birth control are available which are temporary. I explained that sterilization is different because it is permanent.
>
> I informed the individual to be sterilized that his/her consent can be withdrawn at any time and that he/she will not lose any health services or benefits provided by federal funds.
>
> To the best of my knowledge and belief the individual to be sterilized is at least 21 years old and appears mentally competent. He/she knowingly and voluntarily requested to be sterilized and appeared to understand the nature and consequences of the procedure.
>
> (Instructions for use of alternative final paragraphs: Use the first paragraph below except in the case of premature delivery or emergency abdominal surgery where the sterilization is performed less than 30 days after the date of the individual's signature on the consent form. In those cases, the second paragraph below must be used. Cross out the paragraph which is not used.)
>
> (1) At least 30 days have passed between the date of the individual's signature on this consent form and the date the sterilization was performed.
>
> (2) This sterilization was performed less than 30 days but more than 72 hours after the date of the individual's signature on this consent form because of the following circumstances (check applicable box and fill in information requested):
>
> __Premature delivery
>
> __Individual's expected date of delivery:
>
> __Emergency abdominal surgery:
>
> (describe circumstances):
>
> > *Physician*   *Date*
>
> ---
>
> *Source:* Reprinted from Code of Federal Regulations, Vol. 42, Section 441.259.

Performing a sterilization on a woman under 21 years old or without the 30-day waiting period does not violate federal law, but the government will not reimburse for the surgery. The hospital or health care facility in which the surgery is done may require that its own consent form be signed just before surgery. This second form is in addition to the form to show eligibility for federal reimbursement.

A consent form is not a contract to sterilize. A patient may revoke consent at any time prior to the procedure. In turn, a physician should decline to sterilize a patient if the procedure is unduly unsafe or if consent is in question. If a nurse informs a physician that the patient appears to lack understanding of the planned procedure, the physician should promptly discuss the surgery with the patient again to reaffirm consent.

PROFESSIONAL LIABILITY

During the past ten years, professional liability cases involving sterilizations have been related to two general sets of allegations: (1) lack of consent (including sterilization complication cases alleging lack of informed consent) and (2) failure of the procedure. The American College of Obstetricians and Gynecologists reported in 1988 that of 1,449 gynecological professional liability claims against its surveyed membership, 9.5 percent involved sterilization failure.[25] The cases discussed below illustrate the types of sterilization claims being made.

Lack of Consent

Some cases allege total lack of express or implied consent to sterilize. In a Maryland case, for example, an unmarried, 25-year-old mother of two boys sued her physician for the unauthorized removal of her reproductive organs. During surgery for a presumed ovarian cyst in 1976, the physician discovered a ruptured left fallopian tube due to an ectopic pregnancy and a large left ovarian cyst. These organs were removed. No complaint was made about this surgery.

During the surgery, the physician decided that the right tube and ovary were not in a "functional condition." He therefore did a total abdominal hysterectomy. The original pathology report did not confirm abnormalities in the right tube and ovary, although at trial the pathologist reported that on re-examination after suit had been filed he noted changes consistent with chronic pelvic inflammatory disease. There was considerable dispute among experts about the defendant's surgical judgment. There was a jury verdict for the plaintiff in the amount of $1.5 million; the court reduced the damages to $1.2 million. On appeal the court found for the plaintiff by upholding the jury's verdict that a reasonable person, if informed, would not have consented to the surgery that was performed in this case.

It long has been held that in a true emergency no surgical consent is required. There may be unusual cases where this doctrine is applicable to a sterilization procedure. More usual are the findings in *Beck v. Lovell*.[26] In 1975, Mrs. Beck entered the hospital in premature labor for the birth of her third child. She and her husband had a known blood incompatibility, but earlier children were unaffected. She and the physician had discussed tubal ligation, but the patient maintained that she had said she would think about it. The physician claimed that he had received her implied consent for sterilization. Upon admission to the hospital, the patient was presented with a blanket consent form, but she insisted that the portion about sterilization be deleted before she signed it. During the surgery, when the physician realized that the patient had not executed a hospital sterilization consent form, he sent a nurse out of the operating room to obtain the husband's consent. He then performed the tubal ligation.

The wife sued for damages over the unauthorized portion of the surgery. While there was dispute about the issue of consent in this case, the court found that the admission consent form (which was in the medical record in the operating room but which the physician had not seen) should have put doubt into the physician's mind about the patient's consent. In any event, the court found that the physician did have some doubt about the patient's consent, because he sought to obtain the husband's consent. The husband's consent, however, was ineffective since there was no emergency. The appeals court awarded the plaintiff $25,000 in damages against the physician.

The court found that the nursing staff was not negligent in its care of the patient.[27] Specifically, it noted that the nurses had discharged their duties to the patient by placing the admitting blanket consent form in the chart where the physician could find it and later by doing as the physician requested in taking the standard form to the husband for signature. Other juries might find against the hospital, if it appeared from the facts that the nurses should have informed the physician not only of the absence of the required form but also of the admitting nurse's discussion with the patient in which the patient had expressed her active refusal to consent to sterilization.

Sterilization Complications

Complications of a sterilization procedure are known to occur occasionally even in the absence of negligence, but cases alleging, for example, negligent bowel perforation are often hard to prove. Along with the standard allegations of negligence, a female patient may claim that she was not warned that bowel perforation could occur. She will then claim that had she known of that possibility, she would not have undergone the procedure. Even if the original bowel damage was not negligently produced, a failure to recognize and repair the damage promptly may be considered negligence.

Recent literature includes several case studies. One discusses a patient who underwent a laparoscopic bilateral tubal ligation at 8 A.M. on Friday without apparent complications and was discharged. She was seen in the emergency room that night at 9 P.M.; her own physician had signed out for the weekend. She was given pain medication in the emergency room and discharged. She called three times Saturday and finally admitted herself to the hospital on Saturday night. Though she was seen by a general surgeon, she did not undergo exploratory laparotomy until Monday. A burn of the terminal ileus was repaired but perforated several days later. The patient was returned to the operating room three more times for the draining of multiple abscesses.

In the subsequent lawsuit, the emergency room physician admitted he had never seen a laparoscopy. The weekend physician delayed in treating the patient, because the patient was "nervous" and her blood work was normal, although the physician knew that bowel damage should be suspected in laparoscopic tubal ligation patients who do not improve. The general surgeon was later dropped from the case. The author notes that the case is a difficult one to defend.[28] He calls it the "beware of weekend complications" case, because the surgery was done on a Friday by a surgeon who was not covering the weekend. Any physician who agrees to manage surgical cases must be familiar with and attentive to possible complications.

Failure of Sterilization

There have been numerous cases alleging the negligent failure to sterilize. The cases are often called wrongful conception or wrongful birth actions. The damages, which include the pain, suffering, and expense of childbirth to the mother and the cost of child-raising expenses, can be quite large in monetary terms. Negligence is difficult, but not impossible, to prove. Proof may come from a subsequent treating surgeon who performs a repeat tubal ligation and who may be in a position to testify about the previous surgery. Proof also may be available from the pathology report that, for example, may show sections of round ligament instead of fallopian tube.

In general, it should not constitute negligence to fail to sterilize if the surgery proves difficult. However, the surgeon should recognize the possible failure to sterilize at the time and discuss this with the patient after surgery so that a subsequent pregnancy can be avoided. Where a tubal ligation involves removal of tissue, all surgical pathology reports should be read by the surgeon. The pathologist's report should indicate the presence or absence of fallopian tube tissue in the specimens.

The states differ as to awardable damages when negligence in the performance of a tubal ligation is proven. In *Ochs v. Borelli* the physician, Dr. Borelli, performed a laparoscopic tubal ligation on Mrs. Ochs in July 1973. At the time, Mr. and Mrs. Ochs had two children, each of whom had an orthopedic problem. A third child was born to them in February 1975. That daughter suffered a somewhat more severe orthopedic condition. The parents sued the physician and alleged negligent performance of the tubal ligation. The verdict was for the parents.

On appeal the physician conceded liability for the surgery and his duty to pay the orthopedic expenses for the child. Before the court was the question of whether he was also liable for the ordinary expenses of child-rearing. The Connecticut Supreme Court held that he was responsible for those expenses reduced by "the value of the benefits conferred on the parents by having and raising the child. Such benefits may be the satisfaction, the fun, the joy . . . which make economic expenses worthwhile."[29] It affirmed the total jury verdict of $106,360, of which $56,375 was for the costs of care for the child's orthopedic disability plus child-rearing costs reduced by the joy of parenthood. Courts in other states have held that the parents cannot recover normal child-rearing expenses. These courts have found that the joy of having a normal child outweighs the financial burdens as a matter of law.

Some of the sterilization failure cases have involved informed consent allegations. For example, a Kentucky court of appeals affirmed a lower court decision in favor of a physician who had performed a tubal ligation.[30] The Pomeroy method was used and was thought to have a low failure rate. The patient had had eight children prior to her sterilization. After the procedure, she became pregnant with her ninth child. A subsequent treating physician testified that a hysterosalpingogram showed blocked tubes and at vaginal hysterectomy both tubes appeared to be closed. The patient and her husband had signed a consent form which stated, in part, that "[e]ven though good results are expected, I acknowledge that no guarantee or assurance has been given to me as to the results that may be obtained." She claimed that the possibility of failure of sterilization had not been discussed. The court held that it was "inconceivable" that a failure rate was not discussed with a woman who had eight children.[31]

A more recent case alleging failure to inform a patient of a 1 percent failure rate occurred in Illinois.[32] After a verdict for the patient, the defendant surgeon appealed. The Appellate Court of Illinois found that the evidence supported a trial court finding that the surgeon should not merely have given the plaintiff a consent form for sterilization without explaining anything. The court held that it would adopt an objective test in consent cases. Thus, it was not enough for the plaintiff to assert at trial that had "she known that the tubal ligation was only 99 percent effective, she would have chosen instead the 90 percent effective birth control pills that made her sick."[33] The court found no objective evidence that a patient in the plaintiff's position would have refused the surgery even had she known of the failure rate. Further, this conclusion was bolstered, in the court's view, by the fact that the plaintiff underwent a second tubal ligation just four months before suit was filed. By that time, the court noted, she surely knew of the failure rate. Since the plaintiff could not prove causation, judgment was entered in favor of the defendants.

Failed sterilization cases have raised questions about the amount of information to which a patient may be entitled before undergoing sterilization. In *Sard v. Hardy*, a Maryland court of appeals ordered a new trial after a directed verdict in favor of a physician.[34] The patient had undergone a cesarean section with an immediate tubal ligation. The court found that a failure rate, particularly an increased failure rate for the procedure following cesarean section compared with tubal ligations at other times, was a material fact to a prospective patient and should be disclosed.

RISK MANAGEMENT

Much of the legal risk in sterilization procedures, as indicated above, has to do with consent in one form or another. As a result, considerable attention should be given to the consent discussion. That discussion should occur primarily with the patient, although, if she agrees, her spouse may be included. As with other surgery, the surgeon who will perform the procedure should be responsible for providing the material information needed by the patient in making her decision. The consent form signifies only that the discussion has taken place. The form is not "consent" per se. Even those authorities who resist the proliferation of separate consent forms for various procedures usually believe that a special consent form for sterilization is worthwhile. The presence of a consent form, particularly one with some detail (including risk of sterilization failure and risks of the particular procedure to be used, such as bowel injury with laparoscopy), is somewhat protective of a physician and health care facility accused of failure to inform. It is not totally protective, however, because the patient still may claim not to have understood its contents.

A nurse may not have an affirmative duty to explore the adequacy of a patient's understanding of a sterilization procedure, but the patient may offer information that possibly indicates a serious misunderstanding. The nurse then must notify his or her supervisor and the attending physician. Anesthesia personnel are also particularly sensitive to consent issues as they attempt to inform the patient about anesthesia risks during their preoperative visits. If there is serious question about the adequacy of consent, it is prudent to postpone the sterilization rather than to proceed.

The patient's consent should be adequately documented. This is most important if the consent form is somewhat brief. It is not necessary to transcribe the contents of a discussion, but it is worthwhile to note the general categories that were discussed. In a possible later case evidence of habit, or what the physician always includes in patient discussions, will be admissible. If the patient has watched, listened to, or read a particular educational device in the office or clinic, the record should reflect that information as well. If a patient refuses to listen to reasonable explanations of risk, the physician should decline to perform the elective procedure.

Occasionally, it may become necessary to do a medically indicated procedure that results in sterilization. The procedure may be necessary because of an emergency situation. The law of informed consent has always made an exception for emergencies. In a genuine emergency, consent of the patient or family member need not be obtained. For example, if a patient bleeds heavily during a vaginal delivery, a cesarean hysterectomy may be required to save the patient's life. If the patient is unconscious (from anesthesia or loss of blood), the surgeon may proceed with the surgery. After the conclusion of the surgery, the surgeon must attend to the documentation of the emergency, along with the postoperative care of the patient.

If the sterilization is medically indicated but not an emergency, the surgeon should avoid a sterilization procedure to which the patient has not previously agreed. For example, if during a cesarean section the surgeon sees evidence of a window in the uterus that would make a subsequent pregnancy unsafe, the surgeon could choose to do a tubal ligation or could close the incision and consult with the patient postoperatively. The surgeon should try to anticipate this type of situation so that a discussion can take place prior to the surgery and consent can be obtained for sterilization should it become indicated. If consent for possible sterilization has not been obtained, the surgeon should do the tubal ligation (which is elective during the cesarean section) only if there is no question about the condition of the uterus and the surgery could not be safely deferred.

Although many patients now remain awake during cesarean sections, they often receive intravenous medications even before the infant is delivered. This fact could render ineffective any consent obtained during the surgery, because the patient may be unable to understand, think, and remember clearly. For this reason, patient's consent to an elective sterilization and her signature on the consent form should be obtained prior to premedication. If the consent discussion has taken place but the form not signed, it is permissible, although less desirable, to have the form signed after premedication.

Careful evaluation and selection both of the patient and of the recommended procedure are advised. The patient should undergo a preoperative examination before admission. Because as many as 30 percent of all pregnancies following tubal ligation are, in fact, conceived prior to surgery, it may be reasonable to consider performing the procedure during the preovulatory phase or excluding the risk of pregnancy through history or pregnancy testing.[35]

The attending surgeon should select the type of sterilization procedure for the patient based on the patient's history and physical examination, the physician's skills, and current professional recommendations.[36] The attending surgeon should be present at the surgery and in a position to view the procedure, even if it is performed by the resident's service. An operating laparoscope with two eyepieces makes this supervision easier. Careful attention should be given to the selection and maintenance of the equipment to be used. The surgery should be documented by dictated note, preferably on the same day while memory of the procedure is fresh. The surgeon should read the transcribed note upon receipt and correct it if it is inaccurate. Once signed, the operative note becomes part of the permanent patient record and the surgeon has, in effect, adopted its contents.

Sterilization procedures do fail even without the presence of surgical negligence. While it is sometimes difficult to face these pregnant patients, it is important for the obstetrician/gynecologist to continue providing good care when requested to do so. Since there is a greater risk of ectopic pregnancy following tubal ligation, this potentially fatal complication must be ruled out. A repeat sterilization must be delayed, of course, if the patient wishes to proceed with the pregnancy, but if she prefers pregnancy termination (and is early enough in gestation), this can be done by the physician or a referral can be made. If the patient requests a repeat sterilization and it is safe to do, the surgery should be performed.

Under these circumstances, some consideration should be given to waiving the surgical fee or accepting insurance reimbursement only. Many health care providers see waiver of a fee as an admission of guilt and they fear that patients share that view. Waiving a fee should not be considered an admission of guilt. Many professionals believe that avoiding unexpected medical expenses for the patient decreases the anger that has been experienced by the patient.[37] In some states, billing flexibility is encouraged by statutes that provide that the failure of a "health care provider to bill a patient for services rendered shall not be construed as an admission of liability and shall not be admissible in evidence as to liability in any trial for malpractice."[38]

SUMMARY

The law of sterilization procedures has changed little in the past few years and is likely to remain substantially unchanged. Issues of professional liability are the most difficult to predict because the circumstances under which patients present vary. However, as the discussion has made clear, certain troublesome patterns recur, and health care providers who attend to these potential risks can minimize them.

NOTES

1. J. Stepan, E. Kellogg, and P. Piotrow, "Legal Trends and Issues in Voluntary Sterilization," *Population Reports* (1981): E74–75.

2. R.A. Hatcher et al., *Contraceptive Technology 1988–89*, 14th ed. (Atlanta, Ga.: Printed Matter, Inc., 1988), 400.

3. H.I. Shapiro, *The New Birth Control Book* (New York: Prentice Hall Press, 1985), 208.

4. Ibid., 208.

5. Stepan, Kellogg, and Piotrow, "Legal Trends and Issues," E78–80.

6. S.J. Gould, *The Flamingo's Smile—Reflections in Natural History* (New York: W.W. Norton Company, 1965), 306–18.

7. Ibid., 308–9.

8. P.R. Reilly, "Eugenic Sterilization in the United States," in *Genetics and the Law III*, eds. A. Milunsky and G. Annas (New York: Plenum Press, 1985): 227–41.

9. *Buck v. Bell*, 274 U.S. 200 (1926).

10. Ibid., 207.

11. *Skinner v. Oklahoma*, 316 U.S. 535 (1942).

12. Reilly, "Eugenic Sterilization," 238.

13. A. Holder, *Legal Issues in Pediatrics and Adolescent Medicine*, 2nd ed. (New Haven, Conn.: Yale University Press, 1985), 279.

14. *Hathaway v. Worcester City Hospital*, 475 F.2d 701 (1st Cir. 1973).

15. Conn. Gen. Stat. Section 45–78q (1988).

16. See *Ponter v. Ponter*, 342 A.2d 574 (Super. Ct. N.J. 1975).

17. See, for example, Colorado Revised Statutes, Sections 27–10.5–128–130.

18. *Frazier v. Levi*, 440 S.W.2d 393 (Tex. 1969).

19. *In the Matter of Mary Moe*, 432 N.E.2d 712 (Mass. 1982).

20. Ibid., 721–22.

21. Hatcher et al., *Contraceptive Technology*, 417, 418–19.

22. R.P. Petchesky, "Reproduction, Ethics, and Public Policy: The Federal Sterilization Regulations," *Hastings Center Report* 9 (October 1979): 29.

23. 42 CFR Sections 441.250–441.259 (1987).

24. See *Peck v. Califano*, 454 F. Supp. 484 (DC Utah 1977) and *Voe v. Califano*, 434 F. Supp. 1058 (DC Conn. 1977).

25. American College of Obstetricians and Gynecologists, *Professional Liability and Its Effects: Report of a 1987 Survey of ACOG's Membership* (Washington, D.C.: ACOG, March 1988), Table 23.

26. *Beck v. Lovell*, 361 So.2d 245 (La. App. 1978).

27. Ibid., 252.

28. R. Soderstrom, "Case Reports II: Sterilization Litigation," *Clinical Obstetrics and Gynecology* 31 (March 1988): 174.

29. *Ochs v. Borelli*, 445 A.2d 883, 886 (Conn. 1982).

30. *Bennett v. Graves*, 557 S.W.2d 893 (Ky. App. 1977).

31. Ibid., 894.

32. *Marshall v. University of Chicago Hospitals and Clinics*, 520 N.E.2d 740 (Ill. App. 1987).

33. Ibid., 742.

34. *Sard v. Hardy*, 379 A.2d 1014 (Md. 1977).

35. American College of Obstetricians and Gynecologists, "Sterilization," *American College of Obstetricians and Gynecologists Technical Bulletin* No. 113 (February 1988).

36. Ibid.

37. Soderstrom, "Sterilization Litigation," 175–76.

38. Conn. Gen. Stat. Section 52–184b.

SUGGESTED READINGS

American College of Obstetricians and Gynecologists: Committee on Ethics. September 1988. *Sterilization of women who are mentally handicapped.* Washington, D.C.: ACOG.

American College of Obstetricians and Gynecologists: Committee on Obstetrics, Maternal and Fetal Medicine. February 1987. *Postpartum tubal sterilization: Appropriate timing after vaginal delivery.* Washington, D.C.: ACOG.

Annas, G. 1981. Sterilization of the mentally retarded: A decision for the courts. *Hastings Center Report* 11 (August): 18.

Bordahl, P. 1985. Tubal sterilization: A historical review. *Journal of Reproductive Medicine* 30:18.

Haavik, S., and K. Menninger. 1981. *Sexuality, law and the developmentally disabled person.* Baltimore, Md.: Paul H. Brookes Publishing Company.

Kaunitz, A., R. Thompson, and K. Kaunitz. 1986. Mental retardation: A controversial indication for hysterectomy. *Obstetrics and Gynecology* 68:436.

Letterie, G., and W. Fox. 1990. Legal aspects of involuntary sterilization. *Fertility and Sterility* 53:391.

Chapter 5

Reproductive
Technologies

5

In 1982 about 8.5 percent of all married couples, or about 2.4 million, were considered infertile.[1] Of these couples about 1 million were afflicted with primary infertility and the rest were secondarily infertile. The treatment of such patients accounted for 1.6 million office visits in 1984.[2]

To meet the needs of the nation's involuntarily infertile couples, medicine has worked rapidly to develop new techniques for the evaluation and treatment of infertility resulting from various causes. Although basic treatments such as artificial insemination have been used for many years, new technologies have been developed. In vitro fertilization and its variations and surrogate motherhood are newer, and they are now established, albeit controversial, procedures.

The rapid development of reproductive technologies, particularly in the past decade, has exceeded the capacity of the legal system to respond in a timely fashion. As a result, there is very little case or statutory law that can be used to guide health care professionals, risk managers, and patients who wish to participate in well-designed reproductive technology services. This chapter addresses several of these technologies and the risk management problems they may present.

ARTIFICIAL INSEMINATION

Artificial insemination is the oldest reproductive technology. The procedure has been used in animals since at least 1322, when an Arab sheik reportedly used cotton soaked in semen from inferior stallions to impregnate his enemy's purebred mares.[3] The first recorded use of artificial insemination in humans took place in 1799, when a physician successfully inseminated a woman with her husband's semen. In the United States, artificial insemination using the husband's semen (AIH) was successful in 1866.[4] An American account of an artificial insemination by donor (AID) appeared in 1909[5] and stimulated considerable, unfavorable public response. Nevertheless, the technology and practice continued to develop.

A study of artificial insemination practices undertaken by the congressional Office of Technology Assessment (OTA) was published in 1988. It estimates that 172,000 women underwent at least one cycle of artificial insemination in a 12-month period during 1986–1987. Of the resulting 65,000 births, 35,000 births were due to AIH and the rest to AID.[6] These numbers can be compared with approximately 100 children conceived each year as a result of surrogate motherhood and 600 children yearly as a result of in vitro fertilization.[7]

The medical literature confirms that infectious disease, including gonorrhea[8] (which can also survive freezing of the semen), herpes,[9] acquired immunodeficiency syndrome (AIDS), and hepatitis, and genetic disease[10] can be transmitted via artificial insemination. Nevertheless, the OTA study confirmed earlier studies when it found that screening of donors is highly variable and periodically insufficient. Nearly 11,000 physicians in the United States at least occasionally provide artificial insemination services to their patients. Donor semen is used in 45 percent of inseminations; 22 percent of all inseminations are performed with semen supplied by a semen bank and 21 percent with semen supplied by a physician-selected donor. Semen banks appear to do a somewhat better job than private physicians in screening donors. Of physicians who primarily use the AID method, 16 percent do not screen the donors for infertility. Although physicians screen most often for infectious disease in the donor, only 44 percent screen for human immunodeficiency virus (HIV) and 27 percent screen for gonorrhea.[11] Fewer than half of the physicians screen donors for family history of genetic disease. Some of these physicians respond improperly to genetic information by eliminating some donors who are no risk and by including other donors who do pose a risk of genetic disease transmission.

Artificial insemination recipients are also screened, often during their infertility workup. An interesting fact is that 52 percent of physicians who regularly perform inseminations do a personality assessment of each recipient. This testing ranges from physician interview and assessment to forms of psychological testing. The data show, however, that 80 percent of the women seeking artificial insemination are accepted. The most common reasons for rejection are nonmedical and include women who are unmarried, psychologically immature, homosexual, or welfare-dependent.[12]

The Law

Artificial insemination has been in common use in the United States since the early 1900s, so both statutory law and case law exist regarding the subject. Approximately 30 states currently have statutes addressing artificial insemination. These laws vary. Only 3 states, Idaho, Ohio, and Oregon, have requirements for donor screening.

The statutes may require that only a licensed physician perform artificial insemination and may require the consent of both husband and wife. Some, but not all, statutes require written consent for the procedure. Some statutes provide that the birth of a child after AID must be reported to a local court where the records are sealed. However, since many physicians who do AID send the pregnant woman to another physician for prenatal care and delivery, compliance with provisions of this kind may be difficult. Most laws explicitly protect the semen donor by providing that he has no rights to the child. Finally, statutes usually provide that the child born after an artificial insemination to which the husband consented is legitimate.[13]

In states where there are no statutes, and often even in states where there are, courts have become involved in the legal questions. The earliest legal question to arise involved whether the child born after a donor insemination was the product of adultery by the wife or the legitimate child of the marriage. Court decisions early in this century found that the child was illegitimate and relieved the husband of any obligation to support the child. All modern cases have held that children born after

AID are the legitimate product of the marriage as long as the husband consented to the procedure at the time (although some of the surrogate motherhood decisions may disrupt this reasoning in the future). In these cases the courts have found that the husband must support the child. Such questions usually arise during divorce actions where the husband seeks to decrease his child support obligations.[14]

At times, the fact situations have been quite unusual. For example, in *C.M. v. C.C.*, C.M. and C.C. were contemplating marriage but did not wish to have intercourse prior to marriage. Nevertheless, C.C. sought to become pregnant and C.M. agreed to donate semen. This he did in one room, and C.C. inseminated herself with a turkey baster in another. After several months C.C. became pregnant. A few months later their relationship deteriorated. After the baby was born, C.M. sued to be allowed parental rights in the child. The court found that at the time of the insemination, the parties had intended for C.M. to function as a father. He was awarded the right to visit and support his child.[15] Subsequently, C.M. brought an action to have his name added to the birth certificate and was successful.[16]

In only one other reported case has a semen donor sued the mother to establish paternity and visitation rights in the child. As in *C.M. v. C.C.*, the trial court focused on the intent of the donor and recipient at the time of the donor insemination. It granted the requested paternity rights but not custody of the child. This outcome was upheld on appeal.[17]

Obviously, these cases raise legal questions in the 1 percent of all donor inseminations performed by physicians using recipient-selected donors. As one commentator has pointed out, where the donor becomes known or was known to the recipient at the time of semen donation, the possibility of successful assertion of a parent-child relationship becomes more likely.[18] This potential legal risk can be in both directions: from donor to mother, as in the above cases, and by a mother against a known donor. None of the reported cases has been of the latter type, except in the somewhat different situation of surrogacy.

Risk Management

Husband-supplied semen is used in 55 percent of artificial inseminations performed in the United States. These procedures raise fewer risk management concerns than those using donor semen, but there are two primary risks. First, the staff must be sure that the husband-supplied semen is handled carefully and not switched with other semen intended for another patient. Although generally husband-supplied semen can be easily replaced if it is improperly handled, some husband semen has been frozen prior to irreversible sterilization. This makes the semen irreplaceable and damages can be proven. For example, in 1987 a couple brought suit when semen stored for this reason was thawed during transit from the cryobank to the site of insemination.[19]

Second, when physicians treat the semen before use by centrifuge or other technique or choose to use intrauterine insemination, recent medical literature should be used to determine proper technique, equipment, and safeguards. The patient should be informed of any risks associated with the technique of artificial insemination. Under the usual circumstances most physicians do not require a signed consent form for AIH.

Several organizations have issued guidelines for use in artificial insemination practices. These include the American Association of Tissue Banks and the American Fertility Society.[20,21] The American College of Obstetricians and Gynecologists has adopted the guidelines from the American Fertility Society. In early 1988 the Centers for Disease Control and the Food and Drug Administration issued recommendations having to do with HIV testing. The recommendations are similar to those promulgated by the American Fertility Society and suggest that practitioners use only frozen donor semen. The donor should be tested for HIV upon donation and then tested six months later; both tests should be negative before the frozen semen is used.[22]

Health care providers who furnish artificial insemination services to patients should be aware of laws in their jurisdictions and recommendations in the literature from organizations with special expertise in the field. Both sources are helpful in organizing and running a service, although it is unwise for a physician or nurse to give legal advice about the status of a donor or the child. Providing the patient with a copy of the statute, if any, is acceptable. Where the recommendations are very specialized, as they are, for example, about donor screening for genetic and infectious diseases, they may set the standard of care for the practice. Failure to adhere to standard and widely accepted guidelines may be difficult to defend in a professional liability action alleging that the patient (and possibly her infant) contracted HIV from a physician-selected donor.

Consent for artificial insemination, particularly by donor, should be in writing even if state law does not require it. Sample consent forms are available from various organizations including the American Fertility Society. The health care provider should obtain consent from the recipient and from her husband, if she is married. While it appears that many physicians decline to inseminate single women, the law does not prohibit these inseminations. It also does not prohibit the use of recipient-selected donors, if the physician chooses to honor such a request. These donors should undergo the same genetic and infectious disease screening as other donors.

There may be some legal risks when the physician personally recruits donors rather than using a semen bank. For example, many physicians recruit medical students and housestaff and rely on these individuals to decline donation if their personal or family medical histories would indicate some risk to recipients. This screening method has proven unreliable.[23] Many physicians also believe that screening for sexually transmitted disease is less necessary when they select donors (who are usually known to them). This is also likely to be an unreliable screening method and one that is difficult to defend.

It appears from the OTA study that practices with large numbers of inseminations each year tend to be more careful about donor recruitment and screening. This is probably because they have organized their practices to ensure that the necessary testing is done. Many physicians in private practice have stopped offering donor artificial insemination, because they do not have the time or facilities to perform adequate donor testing. While infection of the semen recipient is unusual and the risk of birth defects in the offspring of donor inseminations is no higher than the average in the ordinary population,[24] malpractice claims in this area can be very costly.

Medical records of semen recipients should be maintained in the same manner as records of other patients. Most physicians do not identify semen donors in the records. If donor records are kept, they are usually filed in a separate location under code numbers. Limits should be placed on the number of pregnancies from any one donor.[25] A donor should not be used again if an offspring of a prior insemination demonstrates undiagnosed illness.[26]

IN VITRO FERTILIZATION AND OTHER PROCEDURES

In vitro fertilization (IVF), a technique in which an ovum is removed, fertilized in vitro, and placed into the uterus, produced its first living child in 1978.[27] Associated therapies, such as embryo transfer, gamete intrafallopian transfer (GIFT), and ovum donation, have been developed since then. An estimated 160 centers in the United States now offer some or all of these services. In 1987 a total of 14,647 stimulation cycles for IVF or GIFT, along with 490 embryo transfers and 60 donor oocyte transfers, were performed in 96 centers. As a result of these techniques 1,858 babies were born.[28] Despite such advances, the overall pregnancy rate of these procedures is less than 25 percent.[29]

The standard in vitro fertilization, with ovum retrieved and the embryo promptly replaced in the same woman, poses only the usual legal risks related to surgery and to situations in which the resulting infant is abnormal. It is where programs seek to vary the timing and participants that legal and risk management questions should be anticipated. If embryos are to be frozen, control over the conceptus must be clear. The following questions should be considered.

- How long will embryos be kept frozen?
- What if the couple is divorcing and custody of the frozen embryos becomes an issue (a Tennessee Circuit Court judge recently awarded temporary custody to the wife in such a dispute)?[30]
- What if the man dies and his wife asks to have frozen embryos implanted and other heirs object?
- What if the harvested ovum is fertilized with donor semen (the classic AID situation, with the same legal problems)?
- What if ova are taken from one woman, fertilized, and implanted into another (a variation of surrogate motherhood, depending upon which woman is to keep the resulting child)?

Legislatures have not answered these questions through comprehensive statutes. Instead, professional standards are developing in the published literature and are used to guide programs in developing answers to such questions (for example, how long an embryo safely may remain frozen). Some IVF variations are considered experimental by human investigation committees and are subject to rigid oversight.

Risk Management

In general, a patient who undergoes any portion of the IVF, GIFT, or embryo transfer processes, whether as ova donor, embryo recipient, or semen donor (unless the donor is anonymous) should be required to sign a detailed consent form. The form should make it clear that a normal pregnancy or infant is not promised and should answer questions that can be anticipated at the time. For example, in a case where embryos are to be frozen, it is prudent to require that both husband and wife sign a consent form at the time of retrieval, fertilization, and freezing (one form is sufficient). Although the couple need not be husband and wife when later implantation occurs, this consent requirement may minimize any dispute over control of the embryos if the spouses divorce. Circumstances under which embryos may be thawed also should be made clear. For example, a Louisiana statute states that no person, including the gamete donors, may destroy a frozen embryo that appears to be capable of normal development.[31]

Legal assistance in the drafting of consent forms for these reproductive technologies can be useful. It is particularly difficult, when establishing an IVF program, to anticipate liability questions related to the embryo donor's obligations to disclose known family genetic abnormalities. In some states, it may be illegal to pay ova donors, and there are a few laws that restrict or prohibit commercial embryo donations. Since there are many programs now offering IVF and related procedures, sample consent forms have been developed that can be adapted to the relevant state law.

In vitro fertilization and GIFT should be performed by personnel who have adequate training in the appropriate techniques. All personnel should be aware of available professional standards. For example, while there are no laws requiring ovum screening in embryo transfer, the American Fertility Society has issued recommendations in this area.

There are also no legal requirements for screening a fertilized ovum for indications of nonviability, but this apparently is a common technique in IVF programs.

If a patient is harmed during a procedure performed by an unsupervised, inexperienced physician, both the physician and the health care facility may be liable. Care should be taken to maintain the cleanliness of equipment, laboratory space, and operating rooms, as well as the integrity of freezers in which frozen embryos are stored. Embryos that are frozen should be carefully labeled; any error that results in unintentional unfreezing or unintended use in an incorrect patient will be actionable.

SURROGATE MOTHERHOOD

The formal theory and practice of surrogate motherhood developed first in the United States in 1976. By the beginning of 1988, nearly 600 babies had been born through surrogate arrangements.[32] Compared with artificial insemination and in vitro fertilization, surrogacy arrangements have been the subject of considerably more legislative activity. Legislation has been introduced in more than half the states. Statutes have passed in only seven states, but bills are still pending in others. The statutes enacted in Arkansas, Kansas, Nevada, Kentucky, Louisiana, Nebraska, and Indiana have varied from endorsing surrogacy (Arkansas) to voiding all surrogacy contracts (Indiana). Other states have taken middle approaches, such as banning commercial surrogacy contracts. Further legislation is expected.[33]

There also have been several well-publicized cases in which a surrogate declined to voluntarily relinquish the child after its birth despite a contract requiring her to do so. This situation is one variation of a child custody dispute and consistently has been treated by courts in that way. In the face of a custody dispute involving a surrogacy arrangement, courts have found that the contract is at least unenforceable (where it seeks to compel the surrogate mother to relinquish her parental rights). The famous *Baby M* case went further and held that the contract between donor and surrogate was not only unenforceable but totally void.[34] The judge then went on to decide custody and award child support.

Risk Management

A health care provider is ill-advised to begin recruiting surrogates and prospective infertile couples without legal advice specific to the jurisdiction. Surrogacy arrangements can be found in violation of state adoption laws (particularly where private adoption is prohibited) and state baby-selling laws. In New Jersey they may be criminal acts. Angry surrogates and disappointed couples awaiting a child often sue lawyers and other intermediaries who make surrogacy arrangements. A health care provider who brokers a surrogate, evaluates the surrogate's psychological fitness, or presumes to offer legal advice about surrogacy could be among those vulnerable to suit. In one published example a physician agreed to undertake an intrafamily surrogacy arrangement. The physician screened the semen donor for HIV, but did not screen his sister-in-law, the surrogate mother. Unknown to the family, the sister-in-law had been an intravenous drug abuser five years before. During the pregnancy, she was tested and found to be seropositive, as was the baby after birth.[35]

This is not to say that a health care provider should decline to provide prenatal care for a woman who happens to be pregnant, regardless of how she became pregnant. There is no duty to inquire about the parentage of the baby, but a physician or nurse should make no assumption, for example, that the woman's husband is necessarily the father (such as when Rh testing or other evaluation is considered). There should be no more than the usual legal risk for doctors and nurses who provide prenatal care as long as they do not participate in the conception or in any decision about custody of the child after its birth. Most hospitals will discharge a newborn infant only to the mother (or her husband or family member) or to the local child welfare agency or adoption agencies. Once the baby is taken from the premises, a hospital no longer has any legal responsibility for custodial arrangements.

SUMMARY

New techniques to assist the infertile in becoming pregnant are continuing to develop; furthermore, newer ways to use the already developed techniques are also developing. There are legal uncertainties associated with every reproductive technology, and this situation will continue even if legislatures act to address certain of the predictable problems.

Health care providers should not offer legal advice to patients, but instead should refer the couple or patient to a local attorney who is familiar with health law. The standard risk management techniques, including careful attention to the drafting of consent forms, and documentation of patient discussions and care continue to provide the best available protection for the staff.

NOTES

1. U.S. Congress, Office of Technology Assessment, *Infertility: Medical and Social Choices*, OTA-BA-358 (Washington, D.C.: U.S. Government Printing Office, May 1988), 3–5.

2. Ibid.

3. B. Jensen, "Artificial Insemination and the Law," *Brigham Young University Law Review* (1982): 935, 937.

4. Ibid., 938.

5. Hard, "Artificial Insemination," *The Medical World* 27 (1909): 163.

6. U.S. Congress, Office of Technology Assessment, *Artificial Insemination: Practice in the United States: Summary of a 1987 Survey—Background Paper*, OTA-BP-BA-48 (Washington, D.C.: U.S. Government Printing Office, August 1988), 3.

7. U.S. Congress, Office of Technology Assessment, "Statement of R. Alta Charo," 9 August 1988.

8. See, for example, K. Kansen, N. Nielsen, and H. Rebbe, "Artificial Insemination in Denmark by Frozen Semen Supplied from a Central Bank," *British Journal of Obstetrics and Gynaecology* 86 (May 1979): 384.

9. D. Moore et al. "Transmission of Genital Herpes by Donor Insemination," *Journal of the American Medical Association* 261 (1989): 3441.

10. See, for example, C. King and E. Magenis, "Turner Syndrome in the Offspring of Artificially Inseminated Pregnancies," *Fertility and Sterility* 30 (November 1978): 604.

11. Office of Technology Assessment, *Artificial Insemination*, 35.

12. Ibid., 27.

13. See, for example, Conn. Gen. Stat. Section 45–69i.

14. See, for example, *K.S. v. G.S.*, 182 N.J. Super. 102 (1981).

15. 152 N.J. Super. 160, 377 A.2d 821 (Juv. & Dom. Rel. Ct. 1977).

16. *C.M. v. C.C.*, 170 N.J. Super. 586, 407 A.2d 849.

17. *Jhordan C. v. Mary K.*, 179 Cal. App. 3rd 386, 224 Calif. Rptr. 530 (1986).

18. D.S. Kaiser, "Artificial Insemination: Donor Rights in Situations Involving Unmarried Recipients," *Journal of Family Law* 26 (1987–88): 793.

19. *Vegas v. Genetic Reserves Corp.*, reported by Associated Press, March 23, 1987.

20. American Fertility Society, "Revised New Guidelines for the Use of Semen Donor Insemination," *Fertility and Sterility* 49(1988):211.

21. American Fertility Society, "New Guidelines for the Use of Semen Donor Insemination: 1990," *Fertility and Sterility* 53(1990) Supplement 1.

22. U.S. Department of Health and Human Services, Public Health Service, Centers for Disease Control, "Semen Banking, Organ and Tissue Transplantation, and HIV Antibody Testing," *Morbidity and Mortality Weekly Report* 37 (1988): 57–63.

23. M. C. Timmons et al. "Genetic Screening of Donors for Artificial Insemination," *Fertility and Sterility* 35 (1981): 451.

24. M. Verp, M. Cohen, and J. Simpson, "Necessity of Formal Genetic Screening in Artificial Insemination by Donor," *Obstetrics and Gynecology* 62 (1983): 474.

25. M. Curie-Cohen, "The Frequency of Consanguinous Matings Due to Multiple Use of Donors in Artificial Insemination," *American Journal of Human Genetics* 32 (1980): 589.

26. D. Shapiro and R. Hutchinson, "Familial Histiocytosis in Offspring of Two Pregnancies after Artificial Insemination," *New England Journal of Medicine* 304 (1981): 757.

27. P. Steptoe and R. Edwards, "Birth after Re-implantation of a Human Embryo," *Lancet* 2 (1978): 366.

28. Medical Research International and Society of Assisted Reproductive Technology, "In Vitro Fertilization/Embryo Transfer in the United States: 1987 Results from the National IVF–ET Registry," *Fertility and Sterility* 51 (1989): 13.

29. D. Navot and N. Laufer, "Assisted Reproductive Technology: A Clinical Appraisal," *Journal of Reproductive Medicine* 34 (1969): 3.

30. *Davis v. Davis*, Blount Co. Cir. Ct., E-14496/Tenn. 9-21-89.

31. *La. Rev. Stat. Ann.*, Sections 14:87, 121–133 (1987).

32. R.A. Charo, "Legislative Approaches to Surrogate Motherhood," *Law, Medicine & Health Care* 16 (1988): 96.

33. L. Andrews, "The Aftermath of Baby M: Proposed State Laws on Surrogate Motherhood," *Hastings Center Report* 17 (1987): 31–40.

34. *In the Matter of Baby M*, 525 A.2d 1128, 217 N.J. Super. 313 (Super. Ct. Chancery Div. 1987), rev'd on appeal, West Law 6251 (N.J. February 3, 1988).

35. W.R. Frederick, R. Delapenha, and G. Gray, "HIV Testing on Surrogate Mothers," *New England Journal of Medicine*, 317 (1987): 1351.

SUGGESTED READINGS

American College of Obstetricians and Gynecologists. 1984. ACOG releases guidelines for in vitro fertilization clinics. *ACOG Newsletter* (July):10–12.

Andrews, L. 1986. Legal and ethical aspects of new reproductive technologies. *Clinical Obstetrics and Gynecology* 29:190.

Elias, S., and G. Annas. 1986. Social policy considerations in noncoital reproduction. *Journal of the American Medical Association* 255:62.

Gostin, L., ed. 1988. Surrogate motherhood: Politics and privacy. *Law, Medicine & Health Care* 16:1–137. (Note: the entire issue is devoted to aspects of this topic.)

Greenblatt, R. et al. 1986. Screening therapeutic insemination donors for sexually transmitted diseases: Overview and recommendations. *Fertility and Sterility* 46:351.

Katz, B. 1980. Legal implications and regulation of in vitro fertilization. In *Genetics and the Law II*, edited by A. Milunsky and G. Annas. New York: Plenum Press, 351–67.

La Puma, J., D. Schiedermayer, and J. Grover. 1989. Surrogacy and Shakespeare: The merchant's contract revisited. *American Journal of Obstetrics and Gynecology* 160:61.

McGuire, M., and N. Alexander. 1985. Artificial insemination of single women. *Fertility and Sterility* 43 (February): 182.

Strickland, O. 1981. In vitro fertilization: Dilemma or opportunity. *ANS/Women's Health* 3:41.

Strong, C., and J. Schinfeld. 1984. The single woman and artificial insemination by donor. *Journal of Reproductive Medicine* 29 (May): 293.

Preconception and Prenatal Counseling and Diagnosis

6

Congenital malformations are "structural abnormalities of prenatal origin that are present at birth and that seriously interfere with viability or physical well-being."[1] Causes of congenital malformations may be divided into three major groups: (1) monogenic (due to a mutant gene, whether recessive, dominant, autosomal, or gonosomal), (2) chromosomal, and (3) major environmental. It has been estimated that about 7.5 percent of all congenital malformations have a monogenic cause, while about 6 percent are caused by chromosomal malformations.[2] Another 6 percent of congenital malformations are thought to be due to environmental causes in various forms, including maternal infection, maternal illness, chemical and pharmaceutical drug exposure, occupational exposure, and maternal nutrition.[3] An estimated 20 percent of malformations appear to be multifactorial in etiology. In a large percentage of cases there is no known cause.

The science and art of human genetics have developed rapidly since 1956 when researchers determined that a human has 46 chromosomes. Prior to that time the number was thought to be 48.[4] By 1959 researchers had identified an extra chromosome 21 in patients with Down syndrome.[5] Nearly 200 major congenital disorders (not including chromosomal disorders) had been prenatally diagnosed by 1981. These defects include anencephaly and other cranial and brain defects, diastrophic dwarfism and other skeletal system defects, fetal errors of metabolism such as maple syrup urine disease, fetal hemoglobinopathies, and various fetal tumors and cysts.[6] The number and type of conditions that can be diagnosed prenatally increase each year; in September 1987 the list included 380 disorders.[7]

PRECONCEPTION COUNSELING

As techniques of prenatal diagnosis have improved, so have other aspects of genetic science. It is now possible for a couple to seek genetic counseling prior to conception and use this information to make a decision about whether or not to conceive. Patients often request advice or referral from the staffs of women's clinics or gynecology clinics, because many women use these centers for primary care. Private office nursing staffs often assist in the care of both gynecological and obstetrical patients.

Professional liability actions claiming preconception negligence have been permitted in some jurisdictions since at least 1977. In that year the Supreme Court of Illinois considered a case with the following facts. In 1965, the plaintiff's mother, Emma Renslow, was 13 years old when the defendants (a hospital and a physician) transfused her with two units of Rh-positive blood. The defendants were said to have known at the time that Emma was Rh negative but did not disclose the blood transfusion error to her or her family (even though the defendants were aware of the error). In December 1973 Emma discovered she was Rh-sensitized after routine prenatal blood tests. The child of that pregnancy, Leah Ann, was born prematurely with jaundice and hyperbilirubinemia. The suit alleged that the child suffered permanent brain damage. The trial court dismissed the plaintiff's cause of action, but the appeals court reinstated it. In the final appeal, the Supreme Court of Illinois noted that, historically, a negligence action could not be founded upon a duty owed to anyone other than the plaintiff and even the plaintiff had to be legally identifiable and in existence at the time of the injury. The court then went on to modify the notion of "duty" to include the not-yet-conceived child if it was foreseeable that the defendant's conduct would injure such a potential child.[8]

There also have been cases alleging the failure to provide proper preconception counseling. In the first reported case, *Park v. Chessin*, an obstetrician advised Mrs. Park to conceive again after the death of her first child. That child had died five hours after birth of polycystic kidney disease. The obstetrician assured the parents that the child had not died of a hereditary disease and that the chance of another child being born with the same defect was "practically nil." Unfortunately, the risk of a child with the same defect in this autosomal recessive disease is 25 percent. The second child was born with the same disease and died at age two and one-half years. A New York Court of Appeals recognized the cause of action for negligent preconception advice but rejected a claim for wrongful life (see discussion below).[9]

The legal literature includes few cases alleging negligent preconception counseling, but many commentators believe that courts will continue to allow them. These claims have the potential to be especially costly. Although the physician or nurse does not cause the defect, the allegation in this type of action is that the child would not have been born but for the negligent preconception counseling; therefore, the health care provider, it is claimed, should bear the costs of the child's maintenance for life.

Risk Management

Most obstetrical personnel are not experts in genetics, although they may have had some special training in genetic principles. Genetics is a rapidly developing specialty, and it is unlikely that many obstetric personnel (except perhaps perinatologists), continue to remain current in the literature. Questions from patients about the potential teratogenicity of medications (for example, Dilantin) or occupational exposures should be taken seriously and necessary referrals made. The same should be true if a patient asks about a trait, such as deafness, that is present in her family history. Because there are many causes of deafness, both congenital and environmental, obstetrical personnel may be ill-equipped to answer questions accurately about risks of recurrence. If obstetrical nurses or other staff members offer ill-considered or incorrect advice and the patient relies on it, that advice, if negligently rendered, is actionable.

When a patient is referred for genetics counseling, the individual making the referral should document it for two reasons: (1) the documentation clearly indicates the facts relating to the questions asked and the referral made and (2) it may remind the staff to ask the patient about the genetics advice during the next visit.

PRENATAL DIAGNOSIS

There are several techniques currently available for prenatal diagnosis. Some of the techniques are indicators that further diagnostic work must be done, while others can be diagnostic themselves.

Ultrasound Screening

.It has been estimated that 50 percent of practicing obstetricians/gynecologists routinely perform ultrasound examinations in the office.[10] Ultrasound has a "broader application" in obstetrics than in gynecology.[11] In 1984 the National Institutes of Health (NIH) released a statement from its Consensus Development Panel on the use of diagnostic ultrasound imaging during pregnancy. Exhibit 6–1 notes those conditions for which the panel believed that ultrasound could be "of benefit."[12]

Many fetal malformations are potentially detectable through prenatal ultrasound screening. These include anencephaly, renal agenesis, omphalocele, tetralogy of Fallot, and conjoined twins.[13] In addition, ultrasound is used to guide such procedures as amniocentesis, chorionic villus sampling, and percutaneous fetal umbilical blood sampling.[14]

The NIH panel noted in 1984 that routine ultrasound screening is not indicated. Studies of safety and clinical efficacy (perinatal outcome) that were reviewed led to the recommendation that the test be done for medical indications only. A recent publication of the American College of Obstetricians and Gynecologists (ACOG) states that there is still controversy about routine ultrasound screening since recent studies have shown some benefit.[15]

Prior to ultrasound, the patient should be informed of the indication for it, any potential risk, the alternatives to the test, and the procedures used in conducting it. Because ultrasonography is not perfect in its ability to detect fetal defects, the limitations of the scan must be made clear.[16]

Exhibit 6–1   The Use of Diagnostic Imaging During Pregnancy

NATIONAL INSTITUTES OF HEALTH
PRENATAL DIAGNOSTIC ULTRASOUND IMAGING

The Consensus Development Panel of the National Institutes of Health reported that ultrasound could be "of benefit" in the following circumstances:

1. For estimation of gestational age for patients with uncertain clinical dates or verification of dates for patients who are to undergo scheduled elective repeat cesarean section, indicated induction of labor, or other elective termination of pregnancy.
2. For evaluation of fetal growth.
3. For evaluation of vaginal bleeding of undetermined etiology in pregnancy.
4. For determination of fetal presentation.
5. For suspected multiple gestation.
6. As an adjunct to amniocentesis.
7. For evaluation of significant uterine size/clinical dates discrepancy.
8. For evaluation of clinically detected pelvic mass.
9. For evaluation of suspected hydatidiform mole.
10. As an adjunct to cervical cerclage placement.
11. For evaluation of suspected ectopic pregnancy.
12. As an adjunct to special procedures (such as fetoscopy).
13. For evaluation of suspected fetal death.
14. For evaluation of suspected uterine abnormality.
15. For intrauterine contraceptive device localization.
16. For ovarian follicle development surveillance.
17. For use in biophysical evaluation of fetal well-being.
18. For observation of intrapartum events.
19. For evaluation of suspected polyhydramnios or oligohydramnios.
20. For evaluation of suspected abruptio placentae.
21. As an adjunct to external version from breech to vertex presentation.
22. For estimation of fetal weight and/or presentation in premature rupture of membranes and/or premature labor.
23. For evaluation of clinical gestational age when there is an abnormal serum alpha-fetoprotein value.
24. For follow-up observation of an identified fetal anomaly.
25. For follow-up evaluation of placenta location for an identified placenta previa.
26. For evaluation of a history of a previous congenital anomaly.
27. For serial evaluation of fetal growth in multiple gestations.
28. For evaluation of fetal condition in late registrants for prenatal care.

Source: Adapted with permission from "The Use of Diagnostic Ultrasound Imaging in Pregnancy" by National Institutes of Health Consensus Development Panel, *Journal of Nurse-Midwifery*, Vol. 29, p. 235, ©July/August 1984.

The standard of care for an ultrasound examination is developing rapidly. An initial, basic ultrasound examination of a pregnant patient should include an evaluation and recording of fetal number, fetal presentation (during the second and third trimesters), documentation of fetal life, placental localization, amniotic fluid volume, gestational dating, detection and evaluation of maternal pelvic masses (in the first trimester), and a survey of fetal anatomy for gross malformations (in the second and third trimesters).[17] Obviously, screening for fetal position and presentation only can be performed during labor. If limited scans are to be performed at other times during pregnancy, the records should reflect that fact. Even then there may be defects obvious enough to be diagnosable.

Nursing responsibilities during ultrasonography vary. The nurse may be an educator or a coordinator of services or be directly involved with the ultrasound procedure and act as a genetics counselor. As in all other areas, a nurse who undertakes these functions should be well-trained and be responsible for maintaining an up-to-date level of knowledge.

Misdiagnosis in diagnostic ultrasound has occurred. In some cases the fetal abnormality could not be diagnosed by ultrasound, while in others there have been falsely normal or falsely abnormal scans. Studies show that the predictive values of normal and abnormal ultrasound results vary with the expertise of the examiner, the nature of the defect and its prevalence in that geographic location, the use of other screening procedures (such as history and biochemical tests), and the period of follow-up.[18] Misdiagnoses can occur in medical centers because the sonographer, who may be quite skilled, lacks clinical knowledge or lacks access to the referred patient's clinical history and physical findings. In offices the sonographer may have clinical knowledge but may lack adequate ultrasound training.[19]

Legal problems may arise from the failure to diagnose a gross neurological defect, such as anencephaly or hydrocephaly, or when the failure of diagnosis is due to ineptitude of the sonographer or to inadequate equipment. There may be no damages from such an error, however, if the diagnosis could not have been made until well into the third trimester (for example, if the first scan was not done until 32 weeks' gestation). There are more serious problems with a case where serial scans were done and the diagnosis could have been made with enough time for the patient to

Exhibit 6–2   Potential Legal Problems As a Result of Ultrasound Services

1. Nonperformance of an ultrasound study when one was clinically indicated.
2. Inadequate or faulty ultrasound equipment resulting in the failure to identify an abnormality that could have been detected with adequate equipment.
3. Inadequately trained sonographer or inadequately performed scan resulting in the failure to diagnose an abnormality.
4. Failure to transmit ultrasound study findings to the clinician or patient.
5. Failure to transmit limitations of a particular ultrasound study that results in lack of adequate follow-up.
6. Overinterpretation of ultrasound findings resulting in inappropriate follow-up.
7. Complications from an invasive procedure performed with ultrasound guidance.
8. Failure to maintain ultrasound records for a reasonable period of time so that ultrasonic findings can be defended.

have selected a second trimester abortion. Exhibit 6–2 demonstrates the types of difficulties that may be related to ultrasound and give rise to legal action.

An informal study of 120 actual or threatened lawsuits showed that 60 percent involved ultrasound misdiagnoses.[20] Proof of damages in such cases may be difficult. The sonographer did not cause the defect; his or her only error was failure to diagnose it. Four advantages of early ultrasound diagnosis are: (1) the patient can select an abortion; (2) fetal surgery or other intrauterine treatment can be considered with improved chances for fetal survival or decreased effects of fetal defects; (3) delivery can be accomplished in a manner that provides the best outcome for the child; and (4) the parents can make personal plans for the birth of a child requiring extra medical care. Claims related to any of these factors can, with proper proof of negligence, create a serious cause of action.

Risk Management

The development and use of ultrasound in obstetrics is rather recent. Only a small percentage of currently practicing obstetricians have had adequate education in its use during residency training. As early as 1981 the American College of Obstetricians and Gynecologists recommended that a physician should learn ultrasound at a medical center by performing procedures under expert guidance, with further education obtained periodically through postgraduate courses.[21] Recommendations were also made for ultrasound technologists.

In 1984 the NIH Consensus Development Panel recommended "minimum training requirements and uniform credentials for all physicians and sonographers performing ultrasound examinations. All health care providers who use this modality should demonstrate adequate knowledge of the basic physical principles of ultrasound and its equipment, record-keeping requirements, indications, and safety."[22] A recent study demonstrates that these guidelines are not being met by most residency programs in obstetrics and gynecology.[23] Also, no state or federal regulatory requirements exist for office ultrasound and sonographers. Questions of sonographer competence raised by the failure of training creates serious risk management problems. Non-employed sonographers should be required to produce proof of adequate professional liability insurance.

Once the sonographer is competent and credentialed, there remains the question of the proper equipment. The science of ultrasound is developing so rapidly that new ultrasonography equipment may be needed more because the old is almost obsolete rather than because it is worn out. Real time ultrasound scanners are better at detecting fetal movement and heart and respiratory activity; therefore, static scanners are "rarely used" in current obstetric practice.[24] Any office or hospital that is unwilling to expend the necessary capital to maintain quality of service in accordance with the standard of care should not be performing diagnostic ultrasound.

Each patient who undergoes an ultrasound should have an examination that is complete for the indication. For each scan, according to ACOG, "representative photographs or reproductions of that examination should be retained and a report of the findings of the procedure should be recorded. This report should be signed by the individual responsible for the diagnostic ultrasound service."[25] Some sonographers communicate directly with the patient and then with the attending physician, while others send a letter back to the referring professional with the ultrasound results and recommendations. While it may be important to reassure the patient sufficiently, the contents of the communication must reflect any diagnostic uncertainty that may exist. For example, when a chromosomal abnormality is suspected, a karyotype may be the only definitive way to make the diagnosis.[26] The limitations of the individual scan (for example, due to maternal obesity or fetal movement) also must be made clear. The failure to do this may inappropriately reassure a physician or patient with the result that necessary follow-up may not be arranged.

A few patients who have ultrasound evaluations will receive results indicating a problem with the pregnancy or with the fetus. These parents need information and possibly referral. The nurse who provides the necessary services should verify accuracy of the bad news and document the information and follow-up recommendations offered to the patient.

Ultrasound records should be preserved for several years. The statute of limitations for birth injuries to minors varies among the jurisdictions but tends to be longer than the statute for injuries to adults. In the absence of any statute specifying record retention, it is recommended that these records be kept for at least seven years. Every effort should be made to keep the files intact. If an interesting case is used for training or other purposes, copies should be made of the scan photographs and the originals returned immediately to the files.

Any failure to diagnose in an office practice will be revealed at birth or shortly thereafter by the condition of the infant. Communication of this information should enable the sonographer in the office to review the scans to determine if diagnosis could or should have been made during the scans. A referral ultrasound center should consider the establishment of a feedback system for its results as well. A card can be sent, for example, to the referring physician after the delivery should have occurred. This communication need not ask whether any ultrasonic misdiagnosis occurred but rather request confirmation on the ultrasonic findings from the birth.

Amniocentesis and Chorionic Villus Sampling

Amniocentesis was developed in the early 1960s when researchers developed a technique for aspirating desquamated fetal cells from the surrounding amniotic fluid. These cells are used to assess chromosomes in the fetus. Amniocentesis is usually done at or after the 16th week of pregnancy, although in some patients it can be done earlier. Results from the laboratory take 2 to 4 weeks longer. Only 3 percent of the women who undergo amniocentesis for genetic screening receive results that force them to consider terminating the pregnancy.[27] An abortion at 18 to 20 weeks may occur after fetal motion has been perceived by the mother. It has long been considered desirable to be able to obtain material for prenatal diagnosis during the first trimester when abortion, if it is to occur, is safer and easier.

The development of chorionic villus sampling (CVS), or chorionic villus biopsy as it is also known, has taken place primarily since 1980. The procedure was considered experimental at first and its use began at major medical centers under protocols approved by human investigation committees. Most biopsy procedures are done between 9 and 11 weeks of gestation.[28] The tissue samples obtained from CVS can be used to conduct direct chromosomal assays, but they also can be used to grow tissue cultures from which chromosomes are analyzed. It appears that many disorders diagnosed through tissue retrieved at amniocentesis also can be diagnosed via CVS.

Risks to CVS include infection and pregnancy loss. It is difficult to quantify the pregnancy loss, because a certain percentage of pregnancies abort spontaneously during the first trimester without CVS. However, studies show an overall pregnancy loss rate of 3.8 to 4.5 percent.[29] There are also risks of bleeding, infection, rupture of membranes, maternal Rh sensitization, and other perinatal complications with CVS, just as there are with amniocentesis. A recent study confirms that while CVS is safe and effective for diagnosis of cytogenetic abnormalities, it carries a slightly greater risk of procedure failure and fetal loss than amniocentesis.[30] In both CVS and amniocentesis procedures, there is the risk that no appropriate tissue will be obtained or that maternal, not fetal, tissues will be harvested and analyzed so that the procedures will result in errors. With CVS, authorities recommend that both the direct preparation and cultured villi be examined, because it has been determined that discrepancies may exist between the karyotype of the embryo and that of the trophoblast.[31]

Amniocentesis is recommended for women who expect to deliver a pregnancy at age 35 or older. The incidence of Down syndrome in babies born to women in that age group is about 1:365. This rises to about 1:100 live births at maternal age 40 and to about 1:12 at age 49.[32] It is interesting to note that because of declining maternal age, not because of the effects of prenatal diagnosis, the percentage of babies with Down syndrome born to older mothers declined from 44 percent in 1960 to 21 percent in

1978.[33] Because 80 percent of all babies with Down syndrome are now born to women under age 35, some commentators believe that CVS may provide a significant opportunity for detection of chromosomal defects in the fetuses of younger women.

Other cytogenetic indications for amniocentesis include a history of previous offspring with a chromosomal aberration; a chromosomal abnormality in either parent, particularly a translocation; and for determination of fetal sex when a serious X-linked condition may be present that cannot be diagnosed in any other way. Other accepted indications include inborn errors of metabolism detectable by studies of fluid or cells, a risk of neural tube defect, and a risk of certain hemoglobinopathies.

Risk Management

Because of the risks associated with amniocentesis and CVS, especially that of pregnancy loss, patients should be informed of the risks, potential benefits, and alternatives. They also should be clearly informed of the limitations of the studies. Many women are falsely reassured that a baby invariably will be normal because amniocentesis is normal. A consent form should be signed even if the procedures used are not considered under development.

As in other important care areas, patients may refuse recommended amniocentesis, CVS, or other evaluation. They should be told about the potential consequences of refusal, and the discussion should be well documented in the medical record.

While it was once customary to perform amniocentesis without ultrasonic guidance (prior to the common availability of ultrasound), most commentators recommend that ultrasound be used to locate fluid pockets and to help avoid fetal injury during the procedure. Serious fetal injury during amniocentesis is quite rare, but it has been reported.[34] Ultrasonic guidance is also necessary for CVS.

Considerable care should be taken in the handling of the specimens from these prenatal diagnostic procedures. Sample mixing has occurred and has resulted in the patient receiving incorrect information. The worst combination of such errors would result in the birth of an abnormal child and the elective abortion of a normal one.

Percutaneous Umbilical Blood Sampling

Percutaneous umbilical blood sampling (PUBS) done under ultrasonic guidance is now being offered in some medical centers. This procedure provides the perinatologist with direct access to fetal circulation. Indications for fetal blood sampling include a risk of fetal hemolytic disease, a need for a rapid karyotype, intrauterine infection, fetal hemoglobinopathies and coagulation factor defects, fetal platelet abnormalities, and several other fetal conditions diagnosable via blood sampling. Fetal blood gases and acid base status also can be measured. Fetal anemia can be corrected by using a PUBS intrauterine transfusion.[35]

Risk Management

The PUBS technique is still experimental and under protocol in U.S. medical centers. The patient is required to sign a rather extensive consent form that describes the indication for the procedure, the technique, and known complications. The complication rate appears to be acceptably low. Complications include fetal bleeding after withdrawal of the needle from the umbilical cord, fetal bradycardia, and chorioamnionitis.

Maternal Serum Alpha-Fetoprotein Sampling

It now appears to be the standard of care to offer maternal serum alpha-fetoprotein sampling (MSAFP) during pregnancy, although maternal participation remains voluntary. Interpretation of the results depends on maternal gestational age, maternal age, presence of twins, and other factors. The test is a screening tool and cannot be relied upon to detect all neural tube defects. Abnormal results for gestational age usually result in a recommendation for further testing that may include amniocentesis, but this decision depends on the risk of a possible defect. Many centers do not recommend amniocentesis if the risk of pregnancy loss from the amniocentesis exceeds the risk of a defective child.

If the MSAFP result is abnormal, the patient should be informed of the options for further evaluation by a staff member thoroughly familiar with the meaning of the test results. An elevated MSAFP can be associated with a multiple gestation, a fetal demise, neural tube defects, congenital nephrosis, placental abnormalities, and other abnormalities. It also can be associated with an entirely normal pregnancy. Under some circumstances and with significant limitations, the MSAFP can be used to indicate an increased risk of a baby with Down syndrome.

Risk Management

Documentation of discussions with the patient is important, particularly if the patient declines further testing based on the risks of her circumstances. The medical record should also note if the patient was given written material about the indications for and limitations of MSAFP testing.

LIABILITY RISKS IN PRENATAL DIAGNOSIS

Many professional liability lawsuits have been brought against physicians, nurses, and laboratories with allegations involving negligent prenatal counseling or testing. Many of these actions are considered "wrongful life" or "wrongful birth" suits.

Wrongful birth and wrongful life actions are forms of malpractice claims. Plaintiffs must prove negligence as required in more ordinary malpractice cases. Wrongful birth claims are permitted in many jurisdictions. The plaintiffs are parents of an unplanned or unwanted child, and may claim preconception or postconception negligence. Typical preconception negligence cases involve a failure of sterilization or allegations of inadequate genetic counseling (after which the parents conceived a child). Postconception negligence actions may involve the failure of health care professionals to perform prenatal testing or their negligence in the conduct of the evaluation, or they may concern failure of abortion. In either type of negligence claim, the child may be normal or defective. Many of these cases, however, involve the birth of a defective child whom the parents might have chosen to abort had a timely diagnosis been made.

There may be wrongful life allegations in the same lawsuit. A wrongful life claim is made by the child (through the parents as guardians). Such a claim may allege that the deformed child would not have been born had the defendants acted within the standard of care and that the child has had such a miserable life that he or she would have been better off not having been born (that is, better off dead than alive). The majority of jurisdictions that have considered these cases have refused to permit them. These courts have held that the action is contrary to public policy, because it requires the court to value a claim that death, under the circumstances, is preferable to life.

An early example of a case in which wrongful life and wrongful birth claims were combined is *Gildiner v. Thomas Jefferson University Hospital*. Mrs. Gildiner became pregnant in November 1973. Both she and her husband were tested subsequently and were found to be carriers of Tay-Sachs disease. Amniocentesis was performed in February 1974 for the sole purpose of determining if the fetus was afflicted with Tay-Sachs disease. The parents were told in April 1974 that the test eliminated any possibility that the child would be affected. The parents proceeded with the pregnancy. Their son Andrew, born in August 1974, was afflicted with Tay-Sachs disease. The parents sued the physicians involved and the hospital where the amniocentesis was performed. They claimed damages for themselves (a wrongful birth claim). The court found that such a cause of action did exist and denied a defense motion for judgment. The child also claimed damages for himself (a wrongful life claim). In dismissing this action, the court said that the damages claimed were not recognized at law.[36]

In a more recent case, several courts in North Carolina considered a case with the following facts. In 1979 Mrs. Azzolino, then 36 years of age, presented to a clinic for prenatal care. She inquired about amniocentesis. The nurse clinician then proceeded to tell the patient about the nurse's own personal and religious preferences and those of her husband and advised the patient against amniocentesis. She informed the patient of the medical risks without any attempt at a risk-benefit analysis. The patient did not rely on this advice but consulted the physician. Dr. Dingfelter advised her that amniocentesis was not necessary or advisable until the mother was 37 years of age. The parents relied on this information and made no further inquiries. Their son Michael was born at term with Down syndrome.

The parents, Michael's siblings, and Michael sued the clinic, physician, and nurse. The trial court dismissed claims brought for wrongful life and those brought by siblings for wrongful birth, but granted a directed verdict on wrongful birth claims brought by the parents. The appeals court, affirming in part and reversing in part, held that the wrongful life claim could be maintained.[37]

The Supreme Court of North Carolina then considered the case. It held that the wrongful life claim by the child and wrongful birth claims by the siblings were not recognizable causes of action. It went on to hold that even wrongful birth claims would not be recognized in North Carolina, because the legislature had not created these actions. Cases from other jurisdictions where wrongful life or wrongful birth cases are permitted were not persuasive to the court. In the context of this case, the court found that the defendants did not cause the Down syndrome with which Michael was born. Their failure to prevent the birth by offering amniocentesis and providing abortion services, if desired, was not the cause of either the defect or the birth.[38] This finding precluded any discussion of negligent conduct by any defendant.

Wrongful birth claims are permitted in about half of the jurisdictions in the United States, although some states have not considered the question. Where wrongful birth actions are allowed courts have divided on the types of damages recoverable by the parents. Where wrongful life claims are also permitted, damages are not duplicated but divided between the parents' and child's causes of actions. In actions where the unwanted child is normal, three rules of damages have evolved. According to the majority rule, the parents may recover the costs of the pregnancy and birth but none of the costs of raising the child. In other jurisdictions the parents may recover all of the costs associated with the pregnancy plus all the costs of rearing and educating the child, or they may recover child-rearing costs reduced by the value to the family of a healthy child.

In cases where the child is born with congenital defects, a few courts award damages for the lifelong expenses incurred by the defective child, especially if the child will be unable to work. Most courts, however, award damages for the special expenses incurred by a child with the specific defects, that is, money for special education, medical and equipment (such as a wheelchair) expenses, and sums expended to modify a house for special living arrangements required for the disabled child.

Risk Management

Many commentators believe that courts and legislatures are likely to expand at least wrongful birth actions and that the number of claims will increase in the future as techniques in prenatal diagnosis and genetics become more sophisticated. Nurses and physicians who wish to minimize these legal risks must know when a referral for preconception assessment or for prenatal diagnosis is indicated. An individual health care provider need not furnish prenatal diagnostic services if, for example, he or she finds them distasteful. An indicated referral for prenatal diagnosis should be made, however, even if the nurse or physician opposes the techniques because they may induce the patient to select an abortion to end a pregnancy.

The staff providing preconception or prenatal diagnosis must inform patients about the techniques, risks, benefits, alternatives, and particularly the limitations of the diagnostic modalities being used. Specimens should be carefully labeled before sending them to the laboratory. It is helpful for the staff to use a log for tracking specimens to ensure that laboratory results are received in a timely manner. Generally, obstetrical personnel will not be liable for laboratory errors, as long as the selection of the laboratory was reasonable and as long as the obstetrical personnel properly marked the specimen before it was sent to the laboratory.

A health care provider or service that offers prenatal diagnosis may not withhold the result from the patient. Testing results must be transmitted in a timely fashion to the patient or to the referring physician or nurse-midwife, so that the patient may decide the future of the pregnancy based on the test results. The personnel who transmit the results to the patient should be prepared to provide any necessary follow-up information and counseling. All obstetrical personnel who participate in any part of preconception or prenatal diagnosis services should be familiar with current literature and practice regardless of the number and extent of new developments.

Finally, all personnel should attend to the documentation of patient care. The medical record should reflect some discussion when the patient declines recommended prenatal diagnosis. If the patient undergoes screening or testing, the record should show that the patient was informed of the limitations of available tests. Although current technology cannot detect all fetal abnormalities, many patients seem to expect that it will do so and will at least consider blaming the health care provider for any failure to make a timely diagnosis of the problem.

NOTES

1. H. Kalter and J. Warkany, "Congenital Malformations: Etiologic Factors and Their Role in Prevention, Part 1," *New England Journal of Medicine* 308 (1983): 425.

2. Ibid., 426.

3. See Kalter and Warkany, "Congenital Malformations, Part 1," p. 425; "Congenital Malformations, Part II," *New England Journal of Medicine* 308 (1983): 491.

4. W. Nyhan, "Cytogenetic Diseases," *Clinical Symposia* 35 (1983): 2.

5. Ibid.

6. S. Stephenson and D. Weaver, "Prenatal Diagnosis: A Compilation of Diagnosed Conditions," *American Journal of Obstetrics and Gynecology* 141 (1981): 319.

7. D. Weaver, "A Survey of Prenatally Diagnosed Disorders," *Clinical Obstetrics and Gynecology* 31 (1988): 253.

8. *Renslow v. Mennonite Hospital*, 367 N.E.2d 1250 (Ill. 1977).

9. *Park v. Chessin*, 413 N.Y.S.2d 895, 386 N.E.2d 807 (1978).

10. R. Sack and J. Maharry, "Misdiagnoses in Obstetric and Gynecologic Ultrasound Examinations: Cases and Possible Solutions," *American Journal of Obstetrics and Gynecology* 158 (1988): 1260.

11. American College of Obstetricians and Gynecologists, "Diagnostic Ultrasound in Obstetrics and Gynecology," *American College of Obstetricians and Gynecologists Technical Bulletin* No. 63 (October 1981).

12. National Institutes of Health, Consensus Development Panel, "The Use of Diagnostic Ultrasound Imaging in Pregnancy," *Journal of Nurse-Midwifery* 29 (July/August 1984): 235.

13. R.E. Sabbagha et al., "Predictive Value, Sensitivity and Specificity of Ultrasonic Targeted Imaging for Fetal Anomalies in Gravid Women at High Risk for Birth Defects," *American Journal of Obstetrics and Gynecology* 152 (1985): 822.

14. E. Lopez, "Prenatal Diagnosis by Ultrasound," *Journal of Perinatal/Neonatal Nursing* 2 (1989): 34–42.

15. American College of Obstetricians and Gynecologists, "Ultrasound in Pregnancy," *American College of Obstetricians and Gynecologists Technical Bulletin* No. 116 (May 1988).

16. See, for example, B. Benacerraf, W. Miller, and F. Frigoletto, "Sonographic Detection of Fetuses with Trisomies 13 and 18: Accuracy and Limitations," *American Journal of Obstetrics and Gynecology* 158 (1988): 404.

17. American College of Obstetricians and Gynecologists, "Ultrasound in Pregnancy," 2.

18. Sabbagha et al., "Predictive Value, Sensitivity and Specificity," 827.

19. Sack and Maharry, "Misdiagnoses in Obstetric and Gynecologic Ultrasound," 1262.

20. Cited in Sack and Maharry, "Misdiagnoses in Obstetric and Gynecologic Ultrasound," 1260.

21. American College of Obstetricians and Gynecologists, "Diagnostic Ultrasound," 1.

22. National Institutes of Health, "Diagnostic Ultrasound Imaging," 238.

23. J. Ahram, S.J. Feinstein, and H. DePhillips, "Survey of Ultrasound Training in Obstetrics and Gynecology Residency Training Programs in the United States," *Obstetrics and Gynecology* 70 (1987): 3.

24. American College of Obstetricians and Gynecologists, "Ultrasound in Pregnancy," 1.

25. American College of Obstetricians and Gynecologists, "Diagnostic Ultrasound," 1.

26. A. Donnenfeld and M. Mennuti, "Sonographic Findings in Fetuses with Common Chromosome Abnormalities," Clinical Obstetrics and Gynecology 31 (1988): 80.

27. A. Milunsky, "Prenatal Diagnosis: New Tools, New Problems," in Genetics and the Law III, eds. A. Milunsky and G. Annas (New York: Plenum Press, 1985), 335.

28. C. Morgan and S. Elias, "Prenatal Diagnosis of Genetic Disorders," Journal of Perinatal/Neonatal Nursing 2 (1989): 1–12.

29. R.J. Wapner and L. Jackson, "Chorionic Villus Sampling," Clinical Obstetrics and Gynecology 31 (1988): 328.

30. G.G. Rhodes et al., "The Safety and Efficacy of Chorionic Villus Sampling for Early Prenatal Diagnosis of Cytogenetic Abnormalities," New England Journal of Medicine 320 (1989): 609.

31. Wapner and Jackson, "Chorionic Villus Sampling," 342.

32. American Academy of Pediatrics and American College of Obstetricians and Gynecologists, Guidelines for Perinatal Care, 2d ed. (Elk Grove, Ill.: AAP and Washington, D.C.: ACOG, 1988), 236.

33. President's Commission for the Study of Ethical Problems in Medicine and Biomedical and Behavioral Research, Screening and Counseling for Genetic Conditions (Washington, D.C.: President's Commission, 1983), 78.

34. S. Merin and Y. Beyth, "Uniocular Congenital Blindness as a Complication of Midtrimester Amniocentesis," American Journal of Ophthalmology 89 (1980): 299.

35. A. Ludomirski and S. Weiner, "Percutaneous Fetal Umbilical Blood Sampling," Clinical Obstetrics and Gynecology 31 (1988): 19.

36. Gildiner v. Thomas Jefferson University Hospital, 451 F.Supp. 692 (E.D. Pa. 1978).

37. Azzolino v. Dingfelter, 322 S.E.2d 567 (N.C. App. 1984).

38. Azzolino v. Dingfelter, 337 S.E.2d 528 (N.C. 1985).

SUGGESTED READINGS

American Society of Human Genetics. 1987. Policy statement for maternal serum alpha-fetoprotein screening programs and quality control for laboratories performing maternal serum and amniotic fluid alpha-fetoprotein assays. American Journal of Human Genetics 40:75.

Annas, G. 1985. Is a genetic screening test ready when lawyers say it is? Hastings Center Report 15 (December): 16.

Burton, B. 1988. Elevated maternal serum alpha-fetoprotein (MSAFP): Interpretation and follow-up. Clinical Obstetrics and Gynecology 31:293.

Epley, S., J. Hanson, and D. Cruikshank. 1979. Fetal injury with midtrimester diagnostic amniocentesis. Obstetrics and Gynecology 53:77.

Fletcher, J. 1979. Ethics and amniocentesis for fetal sex selection. New England Journal of Medicine 301:550.

Green, J., and J. Hobbins. 1988. Abdominal ultrasound examination of the first-trimester fetus. American Journal of Obstetrics and Gynecology 159:165.

Hammer, R.M., and M.A. Tufts. 1986. Chorionic villi sampling for detecting fetal disorders. *MCN* 11:29.

Hsai, Y.E. 1980. The law and operation of genetic screening programs. In *Genetics and the law II*, edited by A. Milunsky and G. Annas. New York: Plenum Press, 97–117.

Johnson, S., and T. Elkins. 1988. Ethical issues in prenatal diagnosis. *Clinical Obstetrics and Gynecology* 31:408.

Knight, G., G. Palomaki, and J. Haddow. 1988. Use of maternal serum alpha-fetoprotein measurements to screen for Down's syndrome. *Clinical Obstetrics and Gynecology* 31:306.

Milunsky, A. 1980. Prenatal genetic diagnosis and the law. In *Genetics and the law II*, edited by A. Milunsky and G. Annas. New York: Plenum Press, 61–68.

Perone, N., R. Carpenter, and J. Robertson. 1984. Legal liability in the use of ultrasound by office-based obstetricians. *American Journal of Obstetrics and Gynecology* 150:801.

Rhodes, A. 1988. Legal aspects of prenatal diagnosis. *Clinical Obstetrics and Gynecology* 31:233.

Steinbrook, R. 1986. In California, voluntary mass prenatal screening. *Hastings Center Report* 16 (October), 5.

Stoddard, R., S. Clark, and S. Minton. 1988. In utero ischemic injury: Sonographic diagnosis and medicolegal implications. *American Journal of Obstetrics and Gynecology* 159:23.

Chapter 7

The Third Trimester

7

The third trimester of pregnancy follows earlier periods during pregnancy where fetal development and considerable growth have occurred. With advances in pediatrics, babies born during the third trimester are considered viable; many of the smallest survive and do well. During this time the mother may be vulnerable to health problems and to premature delivery, which is considered the most common preventable cause of perinatal morbidity and mortality.

From a risk management point of view, a pregnant woman represents a number of potential risks during the third trimester of pregnancy. Many of these are related to the health and well-being of the viable fetus.

FETAL ILLNESSES AND ABNORMALITIES

Many fetal abnormalities are diagnosed during the first two trimesters of pregnancy. If a defect is not discovered until the third trimester, however, the mother may have no option other than carrying the fetus to term. In most jurisdictions abortion during the third trimester is illegal except to preserve the life or health of the mother, even though the infant may have a defect that is incompatible with life.

Fetal Therapy

Some fetal conditions are potentially treatable in utero, such as erythroblastosis fetalis and obstruction of the fetal urinary tract. Treatment for fetal disorders is not new. Liley reported the first successful intrauterine transfusions for erythroblastosis fetalis in 1963.[1] Since then obstetricians have developed other intrauterine techniques, some of which can be used during the second trimester.

Two general risk management questions are raised by patients with fetuses that could benefit from fetal intrauterine intervention: (1) Can a woman be compelled to undergo intrauterine fetal therapy for the sole benefit of the viable fetus? (2) When a woman accepts this type of therapy, what information should she receive before she can give an informed consent?

Court-Ordered Fetal Therapy

Since a woman can obtain an abortion without significant legal constraints during the first and second trimesters of pregnancy, most experts believe that a court is unlikely to order her to undergo unwanted fetal treatment. For example, a Massachusetts court has refused to order a woman to undergo an indicated cerclage during the second trimester of pregnancy. The request had been made by the husband and refused by the wife for religious reasons.[2]

Despite this, a survey reported in 1987 indicates that at least three court orders for intrauterine transfusion between 20 and 30 weeks have been sought. In two cases, both from Colorado, the court granted the order, and in one case from Michigan the court denied it.[3]

A health care provider may not disregard the objections of a competent adult woman and undertake intrauterine fetal therapy without her consent. The physician must either persuade the patient of the desirability of the procedure or seek a court order. Where the decision is made to accept the pregnant woman's refusal of a procedure, the nurse and physician personnel should document the discussion with the patient. They must give particular attention to the information provided about the consequences of the refusal relating to both mother and infant. Refusal of treatment in obstetrics is discussed more thoroughly in Chapter 9.

Fetal Therapy with Maternal Consent

Many physicians would decline to seek a court order to compel fetal evaluation and treatment, because the techniques require cooperation from the patient and often multiple visits. Thus, most women who undergo fetal therapy do so voluntarily, but they must give their consent. Some fetal surgical procedures are considered experimental, and protocols have been reviewed by the relevant human investigation committee. Whether or not the procedure is experimental, the mother should be told the potential risks of the procedure to herself and her fetus; the possible benefits, but omitting any promise of success; and the alternatives, if any, including the likely course of the pregnancy if the fetal abnormality is untreated. The mother's consent to the procedure should be written and preserved as part of the medical record.

Delivery Choices

Postdelivery survival of fetuses with anomalies varies with the defect and the availability of treatment modalities. Survival also can be influenced by the delivery modality. For example, most commentators feel that babies with open abdominal defects should be delivered by elective cesarean section to avoid disruption of the fetal abdominal contents prior to surgical replacement after birth.

In general, where there is a high probability of neonatal death, many health care providers recommend that the method of delivery be in accordance with maternal wishes.[4] Criteria that may justify nonaggressive management in some cases include (1) a very high degree of certainty that the fetal diagnosis is correct and (2) either a very high degree of probability of death as an outcome of the fetal anomaly or a very high probability of severe irreversible cognitive developmental capacity as a result of the fetal anomaly.[5]

No law requires a pregnant woman to agree to nonaggressive obstetrical management (in which the patient would forego obstetrical interventions designed to benefit the fetus). If nonaggressive management appears to be a reasonable option, it should be discussed with the mother. Any discussions should be thoroughly documented in the medical record; in particular it must be made clear to the mother that the fetus may survive the pregnancy and delivery and be subject to other law regarding neonatal treatment. Possible legal risks in this type of situation may include:

- action before delivery to require the mother to submit to aggressive management for the sake of the fetus (brought by a family member or a third party)
- negligence action, brought by the parents, after birth alleging that the child was born in a worse condition than it would have been if the pregnancy had been managed properly
- negligence action brought on behalf of the child against the mother for her choices during the pregnancy

Each situation in which nonaggressive management is offered should be considered carefully. The potential legal risks then can be better controlled by the health care provider.

ASSESSMENT OF MOTHER AND FETUS

A primary goal of prenatal care is to ensure, as much as possible, that the fetus reaches viability, and hopefully reaches term, before delivery occurs or becomes necessary. Recommendations for assessment and treatment of the potential and actual high-risk maternity patient are changing rapidly. This places a burden on all health care providers who are responsible for the care of pregnant women, because they are expected to be aware of and conform to changes in practice. The Nurses' Association of the American College of Obstetricians and Gynecologists (NAACOG), for example, has stated that intrapartum nurses are expected to acquire the information and skill to care for at least common high-risk conditions, such as pregnancy-induced hypertension, third trimester bleeding, and diabetes, even though a high-risk patient may be encountered infrequently.[6] Education is available from the literature and from in-service and continuing nursing and medical education programs.

Nonstress and stress testing are now widely used for fetal evaluation in both office and hospital settings. As in other situations where fetal monitoring is undertaken, the staff responsible for conducting the tests and interpreting the results should be trained and experienced. Misinterpretation of ominous findings or the failure to evaluate further any questionable findings may be actionable if the fetus appears to have suffered harm. Strips from nonstress and stress testing should be retained for later evaluation just as are intrapartum monitoring strips.

Once a patient in active labor arrives in the emergency department of a hospital, federal law restricts the ability of the hospital to transfer that patient to another facility. A provision in the Social Security Act provides that a patient who is in active labor (defined as a time at which delivery is imminent, there is inadequate time to effect a safe transfer to another hospital prior to delivery, or it appears that the transfer may be unsafe) must be treated regardless of her ability to pay for the services. The transfer of a woman in active labor (or a person with an unstabilized "emergency medical condition") may take place but only under very restricted circumstances, and only if the medical benefits outweigh the risks of transfer. Violation of this statute may subject a hospital and its physicians to fines of up to $50,000.[7]

In July, 1989, the first case tried under this statute resulted in a $20,000 fine being assessed against a physician. The facts involved an indigent gravida 6, para 5 who had had no prenatal care and arrived in the emergency services of a hospital in Victoria, Texas. She was approximately 39 weeks pregnant, had a blood pressure of 210/130, and her cervix was dilated 3 centimeters with 70 percent effacement. Although the nursing staff felt that a transfer to a hospital 160 miles away was unsafe, the physician signed the necessary documents. After at least 1 1/2 hours at the hospital, the patient's cervix was unchanged, and she was moved into the ambulance. She delivered in the ambulance about 40 minutes later. She and the infant were unharmed and were returned to the hospital in Victoria without further problems.

The Inspector General of the Department of Health and Human Services alleged that the physician in this case knowingly violated the provisions of the statute. The administrative law judge agreed, and the fine was assessed. The physician has appealed.[8]

The position that the Department of Health and Human Services has taken in this case strongly suggests that it intends to take action against hospitals and physicians who attempt to transfer medically unstable or laboring patients. Fines imposed under a statute such as this are usually not insurable.

INTRAPARTUM FETAL MONITORING

Physicians reported in a recent ACOG survey that 45.8 percent of the obstetrical claims against them involved fetal monitoring.[9] NAACOG indicated in 1985 that 26 percent of the incidents or claims reported to its members' insurance carriers involved fetal monitoring problems.[10] Data from the Risk Management Foundation indicate that claims related to fetal monitoring are more expensive to resolve than other types of claims. In an analysis of open and closed obstetrical and gynecological claims, 17 percent were found to involve the failure to diagnose, or delay in diagnosing, fetal distress, and 38 percent of the dollars paid went for these claims.[11]

The professional literature and court cases both make it clear that fetal monitoring need not mean electronic fetal monitoring in all cases. *Guidelines for Perinatal Care* (second edition), published by the American Academy of Pediatrics and the American College of Obstetricians and Gynecologists, notes that the "intensity and method of fetal heart rate monitoring used during labor should be based on risk factors and delineated by department policy." It goes on to note that it has been "shown that intermittent auscultation at intervals of 15 minutes during the first stage of labor and 5 minutes during the second stage is equivalent to continuous electronic fetal heart rate monitoring." Where the patient is at high risk or requires intensive monitoring, the standards recommended are either electronic fetal monitoring or a more frequent schedule of auscultation.[12] NAACOG statements have been revised to reflect these recommendations.[13]

Several cases in the legal literature focus on fetal monitoring. In *Williams v. Lallie Kemp Charity Hospital*, Ms. Williams, who had received prenatal care and had an estimated date of confinement of February 20, 1979, was admitted to the hospital at 4 A.M. on March 8, 1979. The fetus was known to be in a breech position. The fetal heart was auscultated only twice prior to delivery, at 4:30 A.M. and 7 A.M. An electronic fetal monitor was available for a period of time, but was not used. At about 6 A.M., the patient underwent x-ray pelvimetry. Ms. Williams was taken to the delivery room at about 7:30 A.M. where she underwent a complete breech extraction. No Piper forceps were used to facilitate the delivery of the aftercoming head. The baby was born very asphyxiated.

Ms. Williams sued on behalf of herself and her child, who at the time of trial was deaf, blind, and a spastic quadriplegic. The court found the staff liable and awarded $500,000 for the baby (the statutory maximum) and $25,000 for the mother. On appeal the court found that, in addition to other negligence during the case, the "child suffered at least some degree of oxygen deprivation during labor which went unrecognized because of the failure of the staff at Lallie Kemp to adequately monitor this child, either manually or mechanically, in accordance with the clearly recognized standard of care." This standard was set forth by expert witnesses during the trial in accordance with *Standards for Obstetric-Gynecologic Services* in effect at the time the care was given. According to the *Standards*, if electronic fetal monitoring was not used, the staff should have at least monitored the child by auscultation every 30 minutes during the first stage of labor and every 5 minutes during the second.[14]

Although the most recent standard of care for fetal monitoring may not require electronic fetal monitoring for even high-risk patients, some physicians may leave standing orders that all patients are to be monitored. Where these orders are in place, but the nurse fails to follow them and harm to the fetus results, the nurse and the nurse's employer may be liable. For example, consider the facts in *Nelson v. Trinity Medical Center*. In that case the evidence showed that Diane Nelson went into labor at about 12:45 P.M. on November 20, 1982. She and her husband left their North Dakota home and drove to Minot for delivery as planned. During the drive Mrs. Nelson noted that the frequency of contractions increased, and she developed abdominal pain.

Upon admission to the medical center, Mrs. Nelson told Nurse Orr about her pain and contractions. The attending physicians had left standing orders that all their patients were to be placed on an electronic fetal monitor. Nurse Orr believed that both of the center's monitors were in use, but she did not check. Later evidence confirmed that one monitor was available. The opinion does not indicate how often the fetal heart tones were auscultated, but a monitor applied at 5:07 P.M. revealed fetal distress. A cesarean section was performed. The child showed extensive brain damage, with an IQ no greater than 15, and inability to control even basic bodily functions.

The family sued the physician and the medical center as employer of the nurse. The physician settled his portion of the case prior to trial (for a sum undisclosed in the opinion), and the trial proceeded against the hospital. The plaintiff argued that the fetal distress had been caused by a placental abruption. The fetal distress, it was argued, could have been diagnosed by the nurse using a fetal monitor, and the abruption could have been diagnosed by a reasonable physical examination of the mother. The jury found for the plaintiff and awarded damages of $7,080,000 (later reduced to $5,680,000). On appeal the Supreme Court of North Dakota noted that the nurse acted independently of the physician even when she was following his orders, so he was not liable for her actions. The hospital was found liable, and the court affirmed the verdict.[15]

In these cases the standard of care is set by testimony from health care providers, physicians, and nurses and is based on current literature and practice. Although the standard is not set by the legal profession, judges, or juries, the jury must decide between conflicting expert testimony from plaintiff and defendant. The results of such jury decisions are often used by health care providers to guide aspects of future care.

Although a case where the staff violated a hospital rule may be more difficult to defend, there still may be no liability. For example, in *First National Bank of Chicago v. Porter*, Nurse Ramsey evaluated Jane Toepper on admission to the labor suite at term on January 24, 1978, at 2:15 A.M. The nurse determined that the patient's cervix was thick and undilated, and the baby was at zero station. Fetal heart tones were 132 beats per minute. Mrs. Toepper appeared to be having Braxton-Hicks contractions. She was discharged by the nurse at 2:30 A.M. Nurse Ramsey was not aware of nursing department rules that required a physician to be notified before a patient was discharged. Had the patient been in active labor, Dr. Porter's standing orders would have required the application of an electronic fetal monitor.

The mother then went home but was unable to sleep because of contractions. She called the hospital and was told to return. A few minutes later she called again, but hung up before the telephone was answered. At that time, she ruptured membranes spontaneously. The fluid was meconium-stained. The patient returned to the hospital, and the physician was called at about 5:30 A.M. No fetal monitor was applied, because the nurse believed that auscultation was acceptable under the labor suite protocols. The baby was delivered spontaneously at 5:56 A.M. with Apgars of 7 and 9. Pediatricians felt that the baby was normal in muscle tone, color, cry, skin, and head size soon after birth and then at two weeks after birth. Thereafter the baby suffered at least two febrile illnesses and showed signs of seizures in October 1978.

The child later showed signs of developmental delay and the parents sued Dr. Porter, the hospital nurses, and the hospital. The jury was unable to reach a verdict and was discharged. The court then directed a verdict for all defendants and the parents appealed. The court affirmed the lower court judgment; it stated that the plaintiff had not proved that the physician or nursing conduct proximately caused the baby's problems and that it was more likely that any injury to the child, Jason, was not due to the labor and delivery but was caused by a later illness.[16]

Risk Management

Case law and practice require that where electronic fetal monitors are in use the staff must be trained and able to interpret the findings. Where a plaintiff can show that a nurse assigned to a patient with an electronic fetal monitor in place is not competent to interpret the strip, the hospital may be liable for both compensatory and punitive damages for its failure to have competent nursing staff.[17]

Nursing and physician staffs should be able to use terms, such as late and variable deceleration, properly and should keep in mind that there is a technical description for what constitutes the terms mild, moderate, and severe late or variable decelerations. Proper terms should be used in oral and written communications about heart rate patterns at least when there is no question about the interpretation of the pattern. Where a pattern is subject to interpretation, written communications should describe the pattern but need not characterize it. Actions taken in response to a nonreassuring pattern should be charted in the written record. Where the pattern returns to normal, the staff should chart that as well.[18]

All fetal monitor tracings for each patient should be labeled with the patient's name so that strips do not become lost. It is helpful to have numerals indicating in which order the tracings were generated when there is more than one strip. Some health care facilities prohibit additional writing on the tracings, but in others certain written information is placed on a strip. It is useful to note such information as changes in maternal position that disrupt the tracing temporarily or increases and decreases in Pitocin dose. Pitocin doses should be recorded on the written labor record, along with vital signs, descriptions of contraction patterns, and vaginal examination results. The staff should avoid placing unexplained question marks over, or circles around, possible fetal heart decelerations. These marks may raise questions about whether the staff recognized the pattern as a drop or just questioned its significance.

When questionable or clearly nonreassuring patterns occur on a fetal heart rate strip, the nurse must notify the physician promptly. The written record should reflect that call and, when the physician responds, indicate actions to be taken in addition to the nursing actions. If the physician does not respond promptly, the nurse must follow hospital policy in getting physician help for an emergency. Frequently, another obstetrician on the labor floor will assist until the patient's physician arrives.

The main labor record should contain the written chronological notes from the labor. Maternal vital signs, uterine activity, and fetal heart tones should be recorded on that record despite the fact that some of this information may already be written on a fetal heart tracing. In particular, if an electronic fetal monitor is in use and the uterine activity and heart rate are noted on the labor record, it should be clear that the staff was observing the tracings and continuing to care for the patient. This is especially important since the current *Guidelines for Perinatal Care* requires that the staff observe the fetal heart tracing every 15 minutes during the first stage of labor,[19] and nursing staffs must be able to document that this has been done. In general, the labor record should be able to stand alone if the fetal monitor strip is lost. Some individuals believe that the same information should be written on the fetal monitor strip so that it can also function as the sole labor record. Others believe that this volume of information on the strip is likely to obscure the tracings and also requires the nurse to write every detail in two different places when time may be of the essence.

Every effort should be made to ensure that neither the written labor record nor any fetal monitor tracing become lost. A fetal tracing is often not kept with a hospital medical record and may not be retained as long, but it should be stored in an accessible place. Since the most interesting tracings for teaching purposes are also those strips that may have some legal implications depending upon the condition of the infant, the staff must be sure that these strips are identified with the patient's name and stored in the proper file after the initial review is completed. Loss of fetal monitor tracings where fetal distress is an issue places the defense at a disadvantage, because the implication is that the tracing was so bad that the staff discarded it.

PRODUCT LIABILITY

Complex equipment is used in all medical specialties, including obstetrics. High-risk patients may be evaluated with electronic fetal monitors, ultrasound devices, and various types of uterine catheters, as well as maternal cardiac and invasive monitoring devices for critically ill patients. Medical devices are regulated by the U.S. Food and Drug Administration (FDA) under the Medical Device Amendments of 1976 to the Federal Food, Drug, and Cosmetic Act. These federal statutes are designed to ensure that medical devices, from tampons and tongue blades to Swan-Ganz catheters, are safe and effective before they are marketed.[20]

Where there is a problem with care involving a medical device, two types of legal actions may be brought: (1) a plaintiff may sue for negligence in the operation of the device or (2) a plaintiff may sue under product liability law and claim that the device was defective. Proof of liability in a product case does not require that the manufacturer be shown to have violated a standard of care; that is, this type of case is not a negligence action. Instead, the plaintiff must show that the product was unreasonably defective and that it malfunctioned and harmed the patient. Strict liability of this kind does not require a showing of fault, and the manufacturer cannot avoid liability by showing that due care was used in the design and manufacture of the product.

Product liability cases may be combined with medical malpractice actions. For example, there could be a claim that a catheter broke off during an arterial catheterization and that the staff malpracticed in the retrieval of the piece. In *McGee v. Corometrics Medical Systems, Inc.* the plaintiff alleged that the staff failed to diagnose the fetal distress of his son. As part of the case, he alleged that the fetal monitor was defective because the tape was run at 1 cm/min, which resulted in the fetal heart rate being more difficult to interpret than if the tape had been run at the recommended 3 cm/min. The plaintiff claimed that the monitor should have had a warning on the outside. Corometrics produced the instructional materials that it supplied the staff. The company showed that it was possible to interpret the strip at 1 cm/min, although it was more difficult. The court held that since the monitor was to be operated by experienced personnel, the company was not required to place a warning about tracing speed on the body of the monitor. The case proceeded on the negligence portion of the action.[21]

Risk Management

The staff must be trained to use relevant medical devices and must be sure that the devices are in good working order prior to use. Alterations in a product after receipt from the manufacturer should be avoided. Alterations can void manufacturer warranties and may increase health care facility and provider liability for malfunction. Scheduled and recommended maintenance and indicated repairs should be made promptly and recorded on maintenance logs. When a hospital receives a notice from a product manufacturer that it is recalling a device or a batch of devices, these products should be removed from service immediately.

OUT-OF-HOSPITAL BIRTH

Non–nurse-midwives, as well as lay midwives, nurses, nurse-midwives, and physicians in some states, participate in out-of-hospital births. Some of these occur in licensed birth centers, and others occur at home. The American College of Nurse-Midwives currently has guidelines for the use of its membership and other professionals in establishing home birth services.[22] Other groups also have set guidelines for the establishment of birth centers.

Arizona, among other states, regulates the practice of lay midwifery.[23] Generally, under such regulations the practice of lay midwifery can be proscribed unless the midwife obtains the required license.

Cases involving nurses who practice lay midwifery have been contradictory. For example, a Massachusetts court held that since a statute did not prohibit the practice of lay midwifery, the board of nursing could not prohibit that practice but could discipline a nurse licensee for practicing midwifery without the required certification.[24] A contrary opinion was rendered in a Tennessee case. Tennessee also does not regulate lay midwifery, and there a court held that a nurse was not practicing nursing when she was working as a lay midwife and so she was not subject to the rules of the nursing board.[25]

A physician who wishes to conduct home deliveries is authorized to do so under a general license to practice medicine and surgery.

There is no law in the United States that bans home or out-of-hospital birth as an option for a pregnant woman. Controls, where they exist, are placed on the provider. In some cases this makes it more difficult for a trained nurse to provide services that would be legal if provided by a lay midwife. This should not impugn the skills and motives of the usual trained home-birth attendant, because it is ten times more risky to give birth at home unattended than with an attendant present.[26]

Assuming that the licensure question has been answered, a primary legal concern for providers of home birth services relates to liability for negligence of birth attendants who may be uninsured. In order to prove negligence on the part of a birth attendant, it must be shown that the conduct failed to meet standards set by other similarly trained birth attendants. This may imply a higher standard for a physician than for a lay midwife.[27] It is also necessary for the plaintiff to prove that the infant (or mother) would not have sustained the same damage if the delivery had been performed in a hospital. Finally, home-birth parents are often among the most well-informed health care consumers. As a result, these parents usually are aware of and accept potential risks involved. Anecdotal data indicate that they may sue less often.

Some members of the public believe that home birth attendants should be available to those who seek them. No principle of law, statutory or otherwise, however, can be used to compel an individual health care provider to attend a case at home if he or she declines to do so. In a 1961 case a physician told his patient during her prenatal care that the proper place for delivery was a hospital. She hired a midwife, but she experienced complications during the birth (the infant was a hand presentation) for which the midwife advised medical attention. The patient called several physicians, but none would attend at her home. When she finally did arrive at the hospital after a six-hour delay, the baby had already died. The patient sued the physicians and lost, as the court affirmed a jury verdict in favor of the physicians. It held that the physicians could not be held liable for abandonment under these circumstances.[28] This case might have been decided differently if a health care provider had promised to attend the delivery at home and then refused to do so when complications had already developed.

There is a potential legal risk to the parents if the infant is harmed during a home delivery. Although all early cases held that the mother's duty to provide necessary medical care for the child commences only after its birth, there have been attempted prosecutions.[29] Further, more recent cases have begun to develop an argument that a mother may have a duty to protect her viable child at least during the third trimester (see Chapter 9 concerning refusal of treatment in obstetrics). For example, in 1986, Pamela Rae Stewart Monson was charged with a criminal misdemeanor for contributing to the death of her baby boy by failing to follow her physician's advice before delivery. Mrs. Monson had a known placenta previa and had been told to avoid sexual intercourse, to rest, and not to take illegal drugs. When she began to bleed, she ignored the instructions, took amphetamines, had intercourse, and did not promptly seek medical care. Her son was born with extensive brain damage on November 23, 1985, and died on January 1, 1986. Although charges against the mother were dismissed, some legal commentators believe that child abuse statutes could form the bases for prosecution of parents if they select an option that is harmful to the child. This is a theoretical possibility, but it is not very likely to occur.

There also have been rare actions by children against parents for intentional or negligent prenatal injuries to the children. In one case, a Michigan court permitted a child to sue his mother for having taken tetracycline during pregnancy; the drug had caused dental discoloration in the child. In this unusual case the court held that the woman's decision to take medications during pregnancy was an exercise of her discretion. In order for the mother to take advantage of the usual parent-child immunity from suit, it was necessary for that exercise of discretion to be found to be "reasonable."[30]

Risk Management

Birth centers and home delivery services should be well-organized so as to minimize risk to mother and child and to the health care provider. Qualifications of personnel should be evaluated. If a mother seeks out her own birth attendant who is not part of a service, the mother undertakes this evaluation. Relevant equipment should be available, and plans must be made in case of obstetrical or pediatric emergency. Available physician consultation, where the physician is not doing the delivery, is advisable. It is also required by law in some jurisdictions, but it may be difficult to obtain. As one commentator noted, while home birth may not be illegal, it is still practiced in defiance of established medical authority.[31]

In general only low-risk women should attempt to deliver at home. Therefore, evaluation of the patient becomes an important aspect of the care delivered by the prospective birth attendant. Records should be kept of the evaluation and of the delivery service. These records should include reference to any discussion with the prospective parents about the risks of home birth in general and any risks that are peculiar to the particular couple. Even lay midwives are usually obliged to comply with state laws about postpartum eye prophylaxis and registration of birth, so all birth attendants should be aware of relevant state requirements.

When a patient comes to the hospital after a failed out-of-hospital birth, she deserves the same sensitive care offered to all other patients. Nursing and physician personnel should not make value judgments about parental choices in these circumstances, and medical record charting should be factual.

SUMMARY

It is likely that the events of the third trimester will continue to be extremely important for the health and welfare of mother and infant and, because of that, for the professional liability concerns of the staff. It remains important that patients understand that not every infant will be normal, and that not every poor outcome is a preventable one. Nursing and physician staff should make every effort to document the decisions made in the management of the patient during the third trimester. Since evaluation and treatment of the third trimester patient involves medical devices, nursing staff must be familiar with the machines, devices, and techniques, and see to proper device maintenance and repair. These devices do not substitute for personal and attentive professional care—every health care practitioner must resist the temptation to watch the machine exclusively and fail to integrate clinical findings with device-generated data.

NOTES

1. A.W. Liley, "Intrauterine Transfusion of Fetus in Haemolytic Disease," *British Medical Journal* 2 (1963): 1107.

2. *Taft v. Taft*, 446 N.E.2d 395 (Mass. 1983).

3. V. Kolder, J. Gallagher, and M. Parsons, "Court-Ordered Obstetrical Interventions," *New England Journal of Medicine* 316 (1987): 1192–96.

4. J. Veille, M. Mahowald, and M. Sivakoff, "Ethical Dilemmas in Fetal Echocardiography," *Obstetrics and Gynecology* 73 (1989): 710.

5. F. Chervenak and L. McCullough, "Nonaggressive Obstetric Management: An Option for Some Fetal Anomalies during the Third Trimester," *Journal of the American Medical Association* 261 (1989): 3439.

6. Nurses' Association of the American College of Obstetricians and Gynecologists, *Practice Competencies and Educational Guidelines for Nurse Providers of Intrapartum Care* (Washington D.C.: NAACOG, 1988), 17–18.

7. 42 U.S.C. Section 1395dd.

8. *The Inspector General v. Michael L. Burditt, MD*, Dept. of Health and Human Services, Department Appeals Board, Civil Remedies Division, Docket No. C-42, 7-28-89; Reported in *Citation* 59:109 (1989).

9. American College of Obstetricians and Gynecologists, *Professional Liability and Its Effects: Report of a 1987 Survey of ACOG's Membership* (Washington D.C.: ACOG, March 1988).

10. R. Brescia, "Statement of the Nurses' Association of the American College of Obstetricians and Gynecologists," in *A Forum on Malpractice Issues of Childbirth Proceedings: 1985* (Minneapolis, Minn.: International Childbirth Education Association, 1985), 28.

11. Risk Management Foundation, "Fetal Monitoring Problems and OB Claims," *Forum* 7 (1986): 19.

12. American Academy of Pediatrics and American College of Obstetricians and Gynecologists, *Guidelines for Perinatal Care*, 2d ed. (Elk Grove Village, Ill.: AAP and Washington D.C.: ACOG, 1988), 67.

13. Nurses' Association of the American College of Obstetricians and Gynecologists, *Statement: Nursing Responsibilities in Implementing Intrapartum Fetal Heart Rate Monitoring* (October 1988).

14. *Williams v. Lallie Kemp Charity Hospital*, 428 S.2d 1000 (La. App. 1 Cir. 1983).

15. *Nelson v. Trinity Medical Center*, 419 N.W.2d 886 (N.D. 1988).

16. *First National Bank of Chicago v. Porter*, 448 N.E.2d 256 (Ill. App. 2 Dist. 1983).

17. J. Pheigaru, "Keeping Staff Up on Electronic Fetal Monitoring," *American Journal of Maternal Child Nursing* 13 (1988): 334.

18. "ACOG/NAACOG Issue Joint Statement of Fetal Monitoring," *ACOG Newsletter,* March 1986, 8. Also, Nurses' Association of the American College of Obstetricians and Gynecologists, "Statement: Nursing Responsibilities."

19. American Academy of Pediatrics and American College of Obstetricians and Gynecologists, *Guidelines for Perinatal Care* 67.

20. D. Kessler, S. Pape, and D. Sundwall, "The Federal Regulation of Medical Devices," *New England Journal of Medicine* 317 (1987): 357.

21. *McGee v. Corometrics Medical Systems, Inc.*, 487 So.2d 886 (Ala. 1986).

22. American College of Nurse-Midwives, *Guidelines for Establishing a Home Birth Service* (Washington, D.C.: ACNM, 1987).

23. R. Weitz and D. Sullivan, "Licensed Lay Midwifery in Arizona," *Journal of Nurse-Midwifery* 29 (1984): 21–28.

24. *Leigh v. Board of Registration in Nursing*, 395 Mass. 670, 481 N.E.2d 1347, later app. 399 Mass. 558, 506 N.E.2d 91.

25. *Leggett v. Tennessee Board of Nursing*, 612 S.W.2d 476 (Tenn. App. 1980).

26. G. Hoff and L. Schneiderman, "Having Babies at Home: Is It Safe? Is It Ethical?" *Hastings Center Report* 15 (December 1985): 25.

27. G. Annas, "Legal Aspects of Homebirths and Other Childbirth Alternatives," in *Safe Alternatives in Childbirth*, eds. D. Stewart and L. Stewart (Chapel Hill, N.C.: NAPSAC, Inc., 1976).

28. *Vindrine v. Mayes*, 127 So.2d 809 (Ct. La. App. 1961).

29. *State v. Osmus*, 73 Wyo. 183, 276 P.2d 469 (1954).

30. *Grodin v. Grodin*, 301 N.W.2d 871 (Mich. App. 1981).

31. Hoff and Schneiderman, "Having Babies at Home," 25.

SUGGESTED READINGS

American College of Obstetricians and Gynecologists: Committee on Ethics. October 1987. Patient choice; Maternal-fetal conflict. No. 55.

Chervenak, F., and L. McCullough. 1985. Perinatal ethics: A practical method of analysis of obligations to mother and fetus. *Obstetrics and Gynecology* 66:442.

Elias, S., and G. Annas. 1983. Perspectives on fetal surgery. *American Journal of Obstetrics and Gynecology* 145:807–12.

Enghelhardt, H. 1985. Current controversies in obstetrics: Wrongful life and forced fetal surgical procedures. *American Journal of Obstetrics and Gynecology* 151:313–18.

Frigoletto, F., and A. Nadel. 1988. Electronic fetal monitoring: Why the dilemma? *Clinical Obstetrics and Gynecology* 31:179–83.

Gilfix, M. 1985. Electronic fetal monitoring: Physician liability and informed consent. *American Journal of Law & Medicine* 10:31–90.

Helfand, M., K. Marton, and K. Veland. 1985. Factors involved in the interpretation of fetal monitor tracings. *American Journal of Obstetrics and Gynecology* 151:737.

Hutson, J.M., and R. Pretrie. 1986. Possible limitations of fetal monitoring. *Clinical Obstetrics and Gynecology* 29:104–13.

Nelson, L., and N. Milliken. 1988. Compelled medical treatment of pregnant women: Life, liberty, and law in conflict. *Journal of the American Medical Association* 259:1060–66.

Perry, S., J. Parer, and M. Inturrisi.1986. Intrauterine transfusion for severe isoimmunization. *American Journal of Maternal Child Nursing* 11:182–89.

Thacker, S. 1987. The efficacy of intrapartum electronic fetal monitoring. *American Journal of Obstetrics and Gynecology* 156:24–30.

Yin, L. 1983. What physicians should know about the regulation of obstetric and gynecologic medical devices. *Journal of Reproductive Medicine* 28:3–11.

Chapter 8

The Postpartum
Period

8

The postpartum period may appear, at first glance, to include only a few incidents that require effective risk management, but indeed there are many. Some questions this chapter addresses may be problems only rarely, but the well-informed nurse can keep the real problems to a minimum.

The postpartum period is defined as that period beginning with the end of the fourth stage of labor and ending with the six-week postpartum examination. This period is unique for several reasons and usually includes both postdelivery hospitalization (of varying duration) and several weeks of recovery at home.

Fortunately, most postpartum women recover normally. It is not always possible to predict which women will experience complications. Documentation of care is particularly important during the postpartum period for this reason. Often, very little formal medicine or nursing is involved in caring for these patients and, for that reason, record documentation seems less important. The postpartum patient needs and deserves the same attentive care whether her recovery is normal or complicated. Documentation of that care continues to be one of the best risk management tools.

NURSING ASSESSMENT

While there is considerable variation in normal recovery from both vaginal and cesarean deliveries, there are some physical findings that are clearly abnormal or at least require further observation and collection of data. Postpartum nurses should be carefully oriented to their job assignments. Every patient should be examined by the nurse assigned to care for her. Abnormal findings, such as unusual bleeding or pain, foul smelling lochia, or a temperature, should be promptly reported to the charge nurse or responsible clinician. The presence of these and other abnormalities should be documented in the medical record, along with normal aspects of the examination that are relevant. It is not necessary to chart all normal findings, but if there are abnormal findings, such as hypertension, the nurse should chart associated normal findings, for example, the absence of pretibial edema or significant proteinuria.

A unique feature of the postpartum hospitalization period is that there are two patients. While the pediatrician may be responsible for the care of the baby, the normal infant will often be present on the postpartum floor and under the care of the postpartum nurse. This requires that the nurse be knowledgeable about normal infant appearance and behavior and about significant deviations from normal. Charting of infant feeding, appearance, and elimination are important during this time.

ROUTINE POSTPARTUM ORDERS

Many institutions rely on routine postpartum orders, a phrase referring to a predetermined and approved list of orders for postpartum patients. Instead of writing a list of orders for each patient, the physician or nurse-midwife simply writes the phrase "routine postpartum orders" on the order sheets. While there is no legal barrier to this practice, potential problems do exist. It is important that each health care provider be familiar with the contents of the orders so that there is no misunderstanding about what is ordered for the patients. A copy of the full list of orders should be posted in a convenient place near the area where orders are usually written. If routine orders are used, there must be a commonly understood system for deleting one or two of them at the discretion of the ordering physician or nurse-midwife. If physicians and nurses who carry out the orders cannot agree on the few basic orders that should remain relatively unchanged (for example, vital signs and activity orders), the staff may find it preferable to stop using the orders and request that orders for each patient be written in their entirety.

Routine orders can be used for the normal mother and also for normal nursery admissions. Postcesarean section orders should be written for each patient. Routine orders should be reviewed and revised as necessary, but at least annually. This permits the list to be kept up to date with the hospital formulary and with current obstetrical practice. Physicians must feel free to write orders in addition to those on the routine order list and to write full orders for any patient without referring to the routine orders used in the facility. Nurses should question any ambiguity in patient orders, both because of potential patient harm and because the standard of care requires it.

POSTPARTUM PROCEDURES

Eye Prophylaxis

In 1884 Karl S.F. Crede, a German obstetrician, found that gonorrhea caused blindness in an infant who had become infected as it passed through the birth canal. He then demonstrated that blindness could be prevented by the instillation of a 2 percent silver nitrate solution into the infant's eyes directly after birth.[1] At one time 25 percent of all blind individuals in the United States had suffered from ophthalmia neonatorum. Today, the incidence of gonococcal ophthalmia in the United States is small but persistent. A recent study of infants born between January 1986 and June 1988 at Kings County Hospital in Brooklyn, New York, showed that the disease occurred in 8 of 12,431 infants. Seven of the eight cases occurred in infants of mothers who had had no prenatal care. None of the neonatal cases occurred in the 248 women who had been treated prenatally for positive gonorrhea cultures.[2]

Some physicians and nurses feel that eye prophylaxis is unnecessary for many patients, particularly in areas where the rates of maternal gonorrhea are low and the levels of prenatal care are high. In these areas the risks of neonatal eye damage seem small, and the prophylaxis can have undesirable side effects. However, the law usually requires eye prophylaxis.

Statutes or state health department regulations required eye prophylaxis for the newborn infant in 49 states, the District of Columbia, Puerto Rico, Guam, and the Virgin Islands by 1964. Montana permitted, but did not require, eye prophylaxis.[3] Most of the laws call for the use of a currently approved topical medication applied to the eyes by the health care provider. These laws can be applicable to family members or others who perform deliveries at home.[4] Most of the laws require instillation of the medication "immediately."[5] Others prescribe a time period after delivery during which the medication must be applied.[6]

Some laws require the use of the substance and make no reference to refusal by the parents. Other laws require the prophylaxis but allow the parents to refuse for religious reasons or for no reason. In states where possible parental refusal is addressed, the law may require that a report be filed with the health department discussing the reasons for refusal.[7]

As in other cases where parents refuse medically indicated treatment for themselves or their children, the nurse or physician must make a decision about whether to honor the refusal. If, after necessary discussion about the risks of blindness, the parents still refuse the medication, the medical record should be adequately documented about the discussion and should include explicit mention of the ophthalmologic risk to the child. It is unlikely that a hospital will obtain a court order over parental opposition for such a relatively minor treatment, but the hospital can choose to do so if the risk to the child is deemed substantial. A serious risk may exist, for example, if the mother had a positive culture for gonorrhea at the 36-week visit and had received no adequate treatment for the disease.

In states where compliance is mandatory, there may be no explicit penalty for failure to comply, or lack of compliance may be a misdemeanor. Further, since ophthalmia neonatorum infections caused by gonorrhea or other organisms are reportable by law to the state health department, a state investigation can take place if an infant develops the disease. Any violation of the state public health code usually is punished by citation against the health care facility.

The staff should be taught how to apply the prophylactic medication. The substance most currently recommended by public health officials should be used. Treatment should be routinely performed by either delivery staff or postpartum staff. Where there is uncertainty about nursing staff responsibility, it is possible that neither staff will administer the medication.

A consent form is not required for this treatment, so many new parents probably are not aware of it. The nursing staff may inform the parents about the treatment and its side effects. Many nurses choose not to do this, especially in states where parental refusal of the treatment is not an option. Some nursing staffs, under pressure from state law requiring compliance and under pressure from parents who are refusing, may simply apply the medication in private and fail to chart it. This solution, while perhaps understandable, is the worst alternative. Not only does it expose a nurse to liability because the medication was given without consent, but it may also expose the nurse to more serious liability if a child becomes blind and the medical record shows no indication that the medication was administered.

There is no reported litigation about consent to eye prophylaxis. Most parents, when told of the medication and its indications, have no objections. If the parents do object, the obstetrician, nurse-midwife, or pediatrician often can be helpful in obtaining consent.

Genetic Testing

Certain states require screening for rare, but potentially treatable, metabolic disorders such as phenylketonuria (PKU). In 1979 and 1980 screening programs for inborn errors of metabolism tested 3,158,521 samples. Nationally, 195 children with PKU were identified, as well as 536 children with hypothyroidism, 25 with galactosemia, 8 with maple syrup urine disease, and 8 with homocystinuria.[8]

Where mandated by the state or recommended by the pediatrician, the screening should be done by the staff in accordance with medical recommendations. For example, PKU testing is done both at discharge from the hospital and at a later pediatric visit. The second PKU test is particularly important, because insufficient protein intake by the baby (if the baby is to be discharged after six hours in an early discharge program) may render the hospital results diagnostically inadequate. PKU blood specimens are obtained by heel stick. Specific consent is not customarily obtained.

The inadvertent omission of mandated or ordered PKU testing can be actionable if the child is damaged by the failure to diagnose the disease early enough to prevent irreversible harm. Similarly, cases have held physicians liable for failure to screen even in small communities where the disease is quite rare.[9] These cases can result in high monetary awards, because damage to the child is irreversible. Also, if the child had been given appropriate and timely treatment, it may have been normal or near normal.

RhoGAM Administration

An Rh-negative mother of an Rh-positive child must receive an injection of RhoGAM within 72 hours of delivery. Processing of maternal and infant blood for typing must be done promptly after delivery to ensure appropriate and timely administration of RhoGAM. Kleihauer-Betke testing may reveal the need for more than one dose. The late administration, or omission, of indicated RhoGAM can have serious consequences for both the mother, who may develop circulating antibodies, and any subsequent Rh-positive fetus.

An Illinois case illustrates the extent of liability that may be possible. The case raised unique questions. A 13-year-old, Rh-negative female was transfused in 1965 with Rh-positive blood. Neither she nor her mother was told of the negligent transfusions, which occurred twice, each involving 500 cc of blood. In December 1973 the woman discovered her Rh sensitization when her blood was routinely screened during her first pregnancy. The lawsuit against those who had performed the 1965 transfusions alleged that the child of that pregnancy was born prematurely by induction and required two exchange transfusions. It was also alleged that the child sustained brain damage. The Supreme Court of Illinois held that the child could maintain a lawsuit against the 1965 hospital and physician for "preconception negligence."[10]

AUTOPSY AND DISPOSAL OF FETAL REMAINS

Unfortunately, some infants are stillborn or die soon after birth. If an autopsy is thought desirable, the staff may ask the parent for permission. New York and certain other states require hospital personnel to request autopsy permission after any death, although families are not required to consent. By statute in most states, the permission of one parent is sufficient to permit autopsy on an infant. If one parent consents and signs the consent form and one actively refuses, the hospital usually encourages the parents to make a joint decision. In general, hospitals would prefer not to do an autopsy if it will distress the family, although the hospital may have the legal authority to do so with one parent's signature. Autopsy permission, where it is given, may be limited in scope to a particular body part or system or may be unlimited. The law permits revocation of autopsy permission prior to the procedure, but the revocation should be in writing and signed by the person who signed the original consent.

In rare cases a stillbirth or infant death may be reportable as a medical examiner's case. By statute and regulation in all states, the medical examiner's office must be notified of deaths under certain limited circumstances. Examples include homocides, suicides, and deaths within 24 hours of arrival at the hospital.[11] The medical examiner may decline to do an autopsy in these circumstances, but if he or she feels that an autopsy is indicated and it is authorized by law, family permission is not sought or required.

Some hospitals make the disposal of an infant's body the responsibility of the parents; others offer the option of hospital burial or cremation. If the parents wish to have the infant buried or cremated privately, they must contact a local funeral director who will arrange to have the body picked up from the morgue. When the hospital disposes of the remains, a parent should sign a consent form. If the mother is ill, the staff should not encourage the choice prematurely. There have been cases, although not necessarily legally actionable, where the mother signs for hospital burial without due thought and later reconsiders her decision. If this happens and the infant is buried along with other infants (as is the custom), retrieval of the body will be practically impossible.

A third option is available at some university-affiliated hospitals. The parents may choose to donate the child's body to the medical school for examination. If this is an option, a parent must sign the appropriate permission. It is generally not possible to transport bodies to out-of-state medical schools, because bodies usually must be embalmed before they are transported over state lines. Most medical schools do not use embalmed remains.

Occasionally parents ask about taking the infant's body home for burial on the family property. This practice is illegal in some places. Where regulations do not address the practice, it may be undesirable for several reasons. The first is sanitation, if the body will be buried near a water supply. Second, recently buried human bones, if found by a neighbor or uncovered by an animal, can precipitate a police homocide investigation to determine the circumstances of the death. Finally, the family cannot take the remains with them if they relocate or make the resting place inviolate as in a cemetery.

While this discussion concentrates on fetal and infant remains, except for the option of hospital disposal of remains, the principles are applicable generally to other deaths as well, including maternal deaths.

CIRCUMCISION

Recently the American Academy of Pediatrics reversed its long-held position that circumcision is not medically indicated, and it now states that there is medical indication.[12] A majority of male infants in the United States are circumcised shortly after birth. A consent form signed by a parent, usually the mother, is necessary to authorize this procedure. The health care provider who performs the circumcision should ensure that the form has been signed. A circumcision performed without consent is actionable as a battery, even though the procedure is performed without complication. Generally, the circumcision should not be performed before the infant has been thoroughly examined by a physician or nurse practitioner and has received vitamin K, because circumcision is contraindicated by certain physical findings (such as hypospadias). While an operative note in detail is not usually required, the health care provider should note in the infant's medical record the fact of the procedure and any complications.

In certain religions, including the Jewish faith, a ritual circumcision may be performed on the eighth day of life. Usually, the infant is home by then, but there may be times when a family requests a ritual circumcision before the infant is discharged. A ritual circumcision may be done by a physician who ordinarily would do the procedure, or the family may request that it be done by a mohel, whom they select. The hospital can refuse to have the procedure done by a nonphysician or permit it to accommodate its patients (especially if the request is made often). The nursing staff should note in the infant's medical record that the circumcision was done at the family's request by the particular mohel. If the child is brought back to the hospital for the circumcision on the eighth day, the health care provider must be sure to note in the child's chart that the procedure was done and by whom.

While family is not usually present for an ordinary circumcision in a hospital, it is the custom for family members to watch a ritual circumcision. There also should be seats available for those who attend the ritual but prefer not the view the procedure.

ROOMING-IN

Infant

When rooming-in first became popular, it was a rigid system that required the infant to remain either in the nursery or with the mother, but did not permit the mother to leave the baby in the nursery when she required rest. Now rooming-in is more flexible. The infant moves in and out of the nursery in accordance with the needs of both mother and infant. This flexibility, combined with visitors on the postpartum floor, has created some security risks for patients, and infants have been kidnapped. Babies should not be left unattended when their mothers leave the room for a period of time to go to the shower or sitz bath. Also, infants have been injured when mothers have fallen asleep with the babies in their beds. In these cases, these injuries usually occur either when a mother rolls on her infant or the baby slips out of a bed without raised siderails.

It is useful for the staff to develop an instruction sheet with safety tips for distribution to newly admitted mothers. Such material can serve as a risk management tool while the patient is hospitalized, but it also can be a safety guide for the mother after discharge.

Spouse

Spouses are encouraged or permitted to stay with the mother until discharge in some health care facilities. This can be done, of course, only when a patient has a private room. The staff should retain the discretion to prohibit spousal rooming-in if the couple is disruptive. This kind of visiting should be considered a privilege, not a right.

VISITORS

Most health care facilities limit visitors to some extent to facilitate the rest and recovery of the patients. Visitors also may be limited for health reasons and should be excluded if there is an infection control risk.

Infection control can be a problem, particularly when sibling visitation is frequent. The staff should ask the parent about a recent history of infectious disease in the visiting child. For example, a child with a recent school exposure to chicken pox may not be ill but pose a substantial risk to the babies and sometimes to nonimmune or immunosuppressed adults. Some facilities have developed a stamp to place in the mother's medical record to show that the appropriate questions were asked before a young child was permitted to visit. Generally, also for infection control reasons, only parents are permitted to handle the new baby. This rule, where it exists, is often seen as an example of hospital rigidity. However, it is designed not so much to protect the infant in question (who will soon be home where the family is free to handle him), but to protect other infants from infections (such as diarrhea) that can spread rapidly in nurseries.

Health care facilities may limit the number of visitors to any patient at any one time. Further, they may exclude visitors who appear intoxicated or are disruptive on the premises. A written hospital policy describing visiting hours and restrictions can be helpful to the staff who must answer questions about visiting and visitors.

ACKNOWLEDGMENT OF PATERNITY

If a couple is married, there is a presumption (rebuttable or irrebuttable depending upon the jurisdiction) that the husband is the father of the child. Where the parents are unmarried, each state establishes procedures by which paternity can be acknowledged voluntarily or alleged at a paternity action. In the voluntary action, the father must usually sign forms provided by the vital statistics bureau indicating that he is the father. This acknowledgment may not be effective until it is also signed by the mother. If the mother denies that he is the father and he disagrees, he may institute a court action to have himself declared the father. If he is successful in this paternity action, he will acquire parental rights of support, visitation, and perhaps the ability to block the mother from giving the infant for adoption. A mother has corresponding rights to institute a paternity action against a male whom she claims to be the infant's father.

Until the paperwork is finished, an unmarried putative father has no legal rights regarding his child. After acknowledgment of paternity is complete, the father, at least theoretically, acquires the rights and responsibilities of legal parenthood. His status then should be similar to that of a noncustodial divorced father. In any legal action brought by a noncustodial father, a court will examine his history of providing child support and his interest in the child.

MATERNAL AND INFANT TOXICOLOGY SCREENING

The frequency of maternal cocaine abuse has increased markedly in the past years, and effects on newborn infants are being reported and analyzed. Other substances, including other illicit drugs and some legal ones such as alcohol, continue to be abused, either singly or in combination. In the past, many health care facilities and providers have had blood and urine toxicology screening performed on patients (both mothers and infants) without special consent because the results were to be used for medical care purposes.

While it is still preferable from a clinical point of view to test for substance abuse, there are potential legal problems with this approach. There have been sporadic prosecutions of women for risk of injury to a minor when either their toxicology screens during pregnancy were positive (usually for an illicit substance or alcohol) or when their infants' toxicology screens were positive and indicated intrauterine exposure.

166 MALPRACTICE IN CLINICAL OBSTETRICAL NURSING

In some states, legislation is now being considered that would require screening of women where there is reason to suspect substance abuse. A positive infant toxicology screen already must be reported to child welfare authorities in other states.

Practice and institutional policies governing the circumstances under which toxicology screening will be done and the form of special consent, if any, to be required should vary depending upon state law. However, despite potential legal risk, many health care providers fear that imposing a special consent requirement on this laboratory test will cause some patients to refuse screening, and make patient care more difficult for providers.

HUMAN IMMUNODEFICIENCY VIRUS

Some states require that human immunodeficiency virus (HIV) testing be done only with written patient or guardian consent, although there may be certain statutory exceptions to the consent requirements.[13] However, in the majority of states, no statute or regulation governs consent for HIV testing for either mother or child. Without state law to provide guidance, health care facilities and laboratories may make rules about consent to testing. Some facilities require written consent by the patient or the guardian before an HIV titer will be run, while others require that the physician ordering the test state that consent has been orally obtained from the patient. Routine testing of prenatal patients (with their consent) has been recommended,[14] but it has not been widely implemented.

A positive HIV antibody test is reportable in a few states, either explicitly or by implication[15] (see Exhibit 8-1). On the other hand, ac-

Exhibit 8-1 States That Require Reporting of HIV-Positive Antibody Testing*

Arizona	Mississippi
Colorado	Montana
Idaho	South Carolina
Kentucky	Wisconsin
Minnesota	

*As of January 1, 1989

quired immunodeficiency syndrome (AIDS), as defined by the Centers for Disease Control, is an infectious disease that is reportable in each state to that state's health department.

Health care employees are now mandated by federal health and safety authorities to use universal blood and body fluid precautions. These requirements are applicable to the care of all patients, including infants, regardless of whether the patient is known to carry HIV. The failure of the staff to use precautions when required by the task being undertaken can subject a hospital to citations and fines by the Occupational Safety and Health Administration and state agencies.[16]

The American Academy of Pediatrics and the American College of Obstetricians and Gynecologists currently recommend that HIV-positive mothers refrain from breast-feeding their infants, even though the risk of viral transmission from breast-feeding is lower than the risk of transmission during pregnancy.[17,18]

DISCHARGE

Discharge against Medical Advice

Periodically, a mother threatens to leave the hospital against medical advice. Unless she is incompetent or committed, the hospital staff will find it difficult to force her to stay against her will. However, if the mother or another family member threatens to take a child from the hospital against medical advice, the situation is quite different. Under the child abuse and neglect laws of all states, parents may not deny their children medically necessary treatment. If the child is being withdrawn from narcotic dependence acquired in utero, for example, and discharge would not be considered safe for the child, the hospital and its personnel would be unwise to discharge the child. State child welfare authorities can be helpful and should be notified in advance by nurses or social workers of any difficult situation that may be anticipated. If the situation is serious enough, the child welfare authorities may choose to get a court order of temporary custody. However, these situations seem often to occur after 5 P.M. or on weekends when child welfare authorities are hard to find.

In some states, there is statutory authority for a physician to hold a child in a hospital without parental consent for a period of up to 96 hours, while the child welfare authorities have an opportunity to conduct an investigation.[19] If no compromise can be reached with the family, such a hold can be invoked and the child kept in the hospital. Security personnel can be summoned, if necessary, to cope with disruptive family members. From a risk management standpoint, such a situation can have legal risk in either direction—there may be risk from the parents if a child is held without authority, but there is also risk in discharging a child before he or she is medically ready. Many hospital administrations would prefer to defend the former legal action because the child has received the needed medical treatment.

The nursing staff in the nurseries and pediatrics units should be very familiar with the facility policies about holding children without parental consent. It is to be hoped that these situations arise infrequently, but when they do they are difficult for staff and family members, and the staff should be prepared.

Early Discharge Programs

Some facilities have developed early discharge programs in which eligible mothers and infants can be discharged from 4 to 24 hours after birth. These programs should be carefully designed with the literature in mind; there are now reports of programs indicating appropriate discharge criteria and follow-up procedures. When a program has been established, the criteria should be followed carefully. In any lawsuit brought for harm sustained from premature discharge of mother or infant, the possibility that the entire early discharge program will be criticized is slight. Instead, the allegation is more likely to be that the patient did not meet the discharge criteria and was discharged improperly. Most risk managers feel that a well-run early discharge program confers little additional legal risk and has real advantages for patient and hospital.

Discharge Instructions

The importance of discharge instructions has increased, because patients are discharged more quickly after delivery than in the past. Particularly important are the instructions most relevant to the condition of the mother and baby. For example, where the pair are discharged under an early discharge program, the literature shows that most infant readmissions are for hyperbilirubinemia. Therefore, attention must be given to instructions about the baby's skin color and irritability. Instructions for observation and care of a circumcision, where appropriate, are also important.

Printed instruction sheets distributed to patients should contain information that is generally acceptable. They also should contain a section for additional instruction as needed. A checklist can be used to show that each patient has received an instruction sheet. Whether or not printed instruction sheets are used, the nurse, at a minimum, must chart that instructions were given. It is not necessary to chart every instruction about every aspect of care. Many hospitals use discharge instruction forms to be completed by the nursing staff. These include space for charting of medications prescribed and a general description of discharge instructions about bleeding, fever, and follow-up appointments.

POSTDISCHARGE TELEPHONE CALLS

When telephone calls are made to a patient for medical reasons, the fact and content of each call should be charted in the relevant hospital or office record. Similar records should be kept of telephone calls from patients who have questions. Health care providers who take calls at home during the night or over the weekend should be encouraged to keep records of the calls so that notes can be made on the first office day after the calls. Some practices have designed small notepads for telephone calls. These can be used over the weekend and then added to the office record later, thus saving the need for transcription of telephone notes into the record.

POSTPARTUM VISITS

Postpartum follow-up varies with individual practice and the condition of each mother. One or more early postpartum visits may be needed if the patient had a cesarean section or a postpartum tubal ligation, or has had complications. At least, there should be a scheduled visit six weeks postpartum. Documentation of all visits should be complete, because they may be the last visits of the patient to a health care provider for some time.

SUMMARY

The only state statutes and regulations, as indicated in this chapter, with specific applicability to the postpartum period are those governing metabolic testing of the newborn, eye prophylaxis, birth registration (vital statistics), and autopsy. The staff responsible for caring for postpartum patients should be familiar with these provisions of state laws.

Even where there are no state rules, there may be hospital policies on such things as the disposal of fetal remains, infection control, and limitation of visitors. For many other questions that arise during the postpartum period, there probably are not written rules upon which the nurse can rely.

Fortunately, most postpartum women and their infants recover normally. This fact may cause both the physician and nursing staffs to be less attentive. A conscious effort is required to recognize true abnormalities among the wide range of normal findings during the postpartum period. A few aspects of postpartum care should not vary. For example, blood types of all patients must be determined and correctly documented. Failure to note an Rh-negative woman and the corresponding failure to give RhoGAM within 72 hours postpartum can be serious and actionable omissions. To varying degrees, all postpartum patients need education, rest, and proper instructions. Documentation of postpartum care, even when it is mostly educational, is important.

NOTES

1. A. Brandt, *No Magic Bullet* (New York: Oxford University Press, 1987), 15.

2. M. Hammerschlag et al. "Efficacy of Neonatal Ocular Prophylaxis for the Prevention of Chlamydial and Gonococcal Conjunctivitis," *New England Journal of Medicine* 320 (1989): 769.

3. P. Barsam, "Specific Prophylaxis of Gonorrheal Ophthalmia Neonatorum," *New England Journal of Medicine* 274 (1964): 731.

4. See *Conn. Gen. Stat.* Section 19a–216 requiring compliance by "the person in attendance at any birth."

5. See *S.D. Comp. Laws Ann.* Section 34–24–8.

6. See, e.g., *Mass. Ann. Laws* Ch. 111, Section 109A.

7. See *Okla Stat.* Tit. 63. Section 1–511.

8. S. Sepe et al. "Genetic Services in the United States: 1979–80," *Journal of the American Medical Association* 248 (1982): 1733.

9. *Naccarato v. Grob*, 180 N.W.2d 788 (Mich. 1970).

10. *Renslow v. Mennonite Hospital*, 367 N.E.2d 1250 (Ill. 1977).

11. See, e.g., *Conn. Gen. Stat.* Section 19a–406, and *Conn. Agency Regs.* Section 19a–401–9.

12. American Academy of Pediatrics, Task Force on Circumcision, "Report of the Task Force on Circumcision," *Pediatrics* 84 (1989): 388.

13. California Health & Safety Section 199.22 (West 1988).

14. H. Minkoff and S.H. Landesman, "The Case for Routinely Offering Prenatal Testing for Human Immunodeficiency Virus," *American Journal of Obstetrics and Gynecology* 159 (October 1988): 793.

15. W. Curran, L. Gostin, and M. Clark, *AIDS: Legal and Regulatory Policy* (Frederick, Md: University Publishing Group, 1988), 330.

16. Occupational Safety and Health Administration, U.S. Department of Labor, "Occupational Exposure to Bloodborne Pathogens," *Federal Register* 54 (1989): 23042–138.

17. American Academy of Pediatrics and American College of Obstetricians and Gynecologists, *Guidelines for Perinatal Care*, 2d ed. (Elk Grove Village, Ill.: AAP and Washington, D.C.: ACOG, 1988), 152, 158.

18. V. Seltzer and F. Benjamin, "Breast-Feeding and the Potential for Human Immunodeficiency Virus Transmission," *Obstetrics and Gynecology* 75(1990): 713.

19. See, e.g., *Conn. Gen. Stat.* Section 17–38a(d) (1988).

SUGGESTED READINGS

Fekety, S. 1989. Managing the HIV-positive patient and her newborn in a CNM service. *Journal of Nurse-Midwifery* 34:259. (Entire issue devoted to HIV issues.)

Ippolito, C., and R. Gibes. 1988. AIDS and the newborn. *Journal of Perinatal and Neonatal Nursing* 1:79–86.

Lifson, A. 1988. Do alternate modes for transmission of human immunodeficiency virus exist? A review. *Journal of the American Medical Association* 259:1353–56.

Schmidt, S. 1983. Consent for autopsies. *Journal of the American Medical Association* 250 (September 2): 1161.

Shapiro, C. et al. 1989. Review of human immunodeficiency virus infection in women in the United States. *Obstetrics and Gynecology* 74:800–817.

Chapter 9

Refusal of Treatment in Obstetrics

9

Competent adults can, and occasionally do, refuse recommended testing and treatment. The law permits them to refuse and bear the consequences of perhaps their poor judgment, because it is believed that the alternative of every decision being made by some central and presumably wise authority is unacceptable.

Refusal of medically indicated treatment in any specialty is worrisome to the health care provider, because it raises fears that the patient will be harmed by that refusal. Beyond that, the physician or nurse may fear that he or she will be blamed in a lawsuit for the harm if the patient, or the estate in the event of death, claims that the patient did not understand the consequences of the refusal. Even the best application of risk management techniques will not eliminate legal risk in dealing with refusal of treatment cases, but it can help minimize the risk.

REFUSAL OF SCREENING TESTS

The standard of care in obstetrics requires a variety of routine prenatal testing, from venereal disease tests and blood typing early in pregnancy to glucose screening for some patients later in gestation. The American College of Obstetricians and Gynecologists recommends in a technical bulletin that Rh-negative patients receive RhoGAM at 28 weeks' gestation in addition to postpartum if the infant is Rh-positive.[1] These are only a few examples of tests that may be required in obstetrics.

As the law of informed consent and a standard of practice supporting the provision of information to patients have both developed, a few court cases have addressed questions about the kind of information a health care provider must make available when a patient refuses care. A famous California case, *Truman v. Thomas*, discusses these issues. From 1963 until March 1969 Dr. Thomas, a family physician practicing general medicine, was the primary physician for Mrs. Truman and her two children. During those years Dr. Thomas did not do a Pap test on Mrs. Truman. He testified that he had recommended the test but that she had repeatedly declined. On at least two occasions when he performed pelvic examinations, she declined to have a Pap test and stated that she could not afford the cost. The physician offered to defer the cost, but the patient wanted to pay cash.

In April 1969 Mrs. Truman consulted a urologist about a urinary tract infection. During that visit the urologist found that Mrs. Truman was experiencing heavy vaginal discharges and had a very rough cervix to palpation. He referred her to a gynecologist. When she did not go, he made an appointment for her. She was seen by the gynecologist, who in October 1969 discovered that Mrs. Truman's cervix was largely replaced by tumor. It was not resectable surgically. She died of cervical cancer in July 1970 at age 30.

Mrs. Truman's children sued Dr. Thomas and claimed that his failure to perform the Pap test proximately caused the death of their mother. The jury found for Dr. Thomas, and the family appealed. The central issue for the Supreme Court of California was whether Dr. Thomas breached his duty to Mrs. Truman when he "failed to inform her of the potentially fatal consequences of allowing cervical cancer to develop undetected by a Pap smear."[2] In this case Dr. Thomas's office notes did not reflect conversations he testified that he had had with Mrs. Truman. Further, he testified that he had not told her of the specific risk she undertook when she refused the Pap test.

The court held that the doctrine of informed consent applies both to patients who consent to proposed treatment and to those who refuse.

Both, the court held, were entitled to know the material facts and potential consequences of their decisions. The court did not hold that the physician should have performed the test regardless of the patient's wishes, but it did find that Mrs. Truman should have received more information. The court reversed the jury verdict and ordered a new trial. There was a strong dissent by a judge who felt that physicians should not have the "intolerable" burden of having to explain diagnostic tests in detail to healthy patients.

At the retrial of the case, it would have been open to Dr. Thomas to produce evidence that most women of childbearing age were familiar with a Pap test and thus specific information about the risks associated with refusal was not necessary. He also could have tried to show that Mrs. Truman would not have undergone the test even had she received explanations. Further, he could have tried to show that the particular tumor was more likely to have caused her death than other malignancies.

Risk Management

For the purposes of this chapter, it is important to note that at least one court has held that the doctrine of informed consent is applicable to refusal of treatment, just as it is to surgery. While there are no cases on this subject from other jurisdictions, it would be well for nurses and physicians to make a point of informing patients of the specific risks associated with refusal of recommended treatment. Documentation of these discussions is also important; it was missing from the records of Dr. Thomas. It is not necessary to list the risks of refusal that have been discussed (unless a few appear vital). A note that they were discussed will help the nurse or physician recall that such a discussion took place and he or she can reconstruct information that is customarily given.

This strategy of providing information and documentation of the discussion should be applicable when a patient refuses any recommended treatment, whether amniocentesis, genetic counseling, ultrasound, RhoGAM, eye prophylaxis for the baby, or other recommendations. The more dire the potential consequences, the more care that should be taken to inform and document.

CONFLICT BETWEEN SPOUSES

Several sections of this chapter address situations in which the spouses fail to agree and the health care provider is caught in the middle. There have been cases, however, where the spouses conflict and the physician is unwilling to request court intervention. For example, in *Taft v. Taft*, when Mrs. Taft refused cerclage during the second trimester of her fifth pregnancy, it was not the physician who sought court intervention, but Mr. Taft. An earlier Taft baby had delivered prematurely during the seventh month and did not survive. The three youngest children were born after a cerclage was placed earlier in pregnancy. Since the birth of the youngest child, Mrs. Taft had become a born-again Christian and she believed that no harm would come to the current pregnancy. Both she and her husband wanted the pregnancy.

The trial court judge issued an order to compel Mrs. Taft to undergo the surgery, and she appealed. The appeals court found that Mrs. Taft was competent and had refused the surgery. It refused to order her to submit, because she was still in the period of pregnancy during which she could, without her husband's consent, request and obtain an abortion. The court explicitly did not decide questions that could have been raised had the fetus been viable at the time of the request for the court order.[3]

While there may be questions about court-ordered treatment during the final trimester of pregnancy, courts have consistently held that adult women may undergo abortion during the first and second trimesters of pregnancy with relatively few restrictions. Thus it seems unlikely that a court would order a woman to undergo surgery or treatment that could benefit the fetus but which she has refused, at least during the first two trimesters. Mrs. Taft's physician in the above case provided the court with an affidavit setting forth his opinion as a treating physician, but he did not initiate the action.

REFUSAL OF BLOOD TRANSFUSION

Patients may refuse transfusion of blood or blood products for several reasons. They may fear transmission of hepatitis or human immunodeficiency virus (HIV) via the blood supply even though the risk is very slight now that blood is screened. Some patients are Jehovah's Witnesses and refuse transfusion of whole blood, packed red cells, plasma, and platelets. Jehovah's Witnesses usually do not refuse plasma volume expanders such as crystalloids and dextrans. The use of albumin, immune serum globulin, or antihemophilic preparations is left to the conscience of the individual.[4]

There are two general risk management issues that arise when patients refuse blood and blood products. The first is whether the facility or health care provider will seek a court order for transfusion. The second is how to minimize legal risk in the event of a lawsuit later.

Court Orders

The courts have been faced with many cases in which parents, for religious reasons, have refused consent for transfusion for their minor children. There has been uniformity in these decisions; parents have not been permitted to refuse their children lifesaving treatment for religious reasons.[5] For example, in November 1988 the Supreme Court of California followed a long line of cases when it refused to dismiss charges against a mother for involuntary manslaughter and felony child endangerment. In that case Laurie Walker's four-year-old daughter had died of meningitis after her mother treated her illness with prayer therapy in lieu of medical attention.[6]

The results have been much less consistent in cases involving competent adults. When the adult has dependent children, some courts have ordered transfusion for the sake of the family. This result seems slightly more likely, although by no means assured, when the adult is the sole support of a minor child. Generally, however, courts have supported the rights of adult patients without dependents and whose feelings appear unambivalent. In between are the most troublesome situations, for example, the pregnant woman at term who refuses transfusion during a necessary cesarean. The two cases below demonstrate the contrasting results.

In *Crouse Irving Memorial Hospital, Inc. v. Paddock*,[7] the hospital sought a court order for transfusion of mother and infant under the following circumstances. Mrs. Paddock was in the third trimester of pregnancy when it became clear that delivery by cesarean section would be necessary. The mother was Rh-negative, had an anterior placenta, and was anemic; the fetus was diagnosed as hydrocephalic. The parents agreed to the delivery by cesarean section prior to term, but they refused blood transfusion for both mother and infant for religious reasons. The court, without much discussion, affirmed many earlier decisions and authorized necessary transfusion for the baby after birth. To the court, it was clear that Mrs. Paddock was "of sound mind and deep religious conviction."[8] However, it found that she was placing the physicians and hospital in an untenable position by consenting to the surgery but placing conditions on how the surgery was to be performed. "Certainly if the medical personnel are requested to undertake a delivery which will entail incisions and this is known to the patient, the attending physicians must be permitted to stabilize the patient from the resulting loss of blood."[9] The court permitted the medical personnel to transfuse the patient, even after delivery, as necessary to stabilize her condition.

Other courts have found that blood transfusion is not an inseparable part of the surgery itself. In *Mercy Hospital, Inc. v. Jackson*, Mrs. Jackson was admitted in February 1984 in premature labor with an oblique to transverse lie. She had a history of a myomectomy. Cesarean section was recommended for delivery. The patient consented to the operative delivery but declined transfusion for religious reasons. After a hearing in which the patient's views and those of the medical personnel were heard, the circuit judge denied the hospital's request for appointment of a guardian for Mrs. Jackson. The cesarean section proceeded without transfusion, and both mother and baby survived. (The staff had predicted a 40 to 50 percent chance that transfusion would be needed.) The hospital appealed the lower court ruling. The Court of Special Appeals in Maryland agreed to decide the case, because the issues were sure to recur within the state. The court found that a "competent, pregnant adult does have the paramount right to refuse a blood transfusion in accordance with her religious beliefs, where such decision is made knowingly and voluntarily and will not endanger the delivery, survival, or support of the fetus."[10]

Professional Liability

Health care providers who decide to transfuse a patient in the face of an explicit and competent refusal by the patient may face legal action for civil assault and battery or for violation of civil rights. There are few reported cases of this kind, but in a recent Canadian case, now on appeal, a court awarded a member of Jehovah's Witnesses $20,000 for the emotional distress she sustained when she was transfused while unconscious.[11]

Cases like this are difficult for the plaintiff to win, because she must argue that, while she survived, she would have been better off dead, as she would have been had transfusion not been undertaken. The scarcity of lawsuits alleging violated rights should not encourage a health care provider or facility to believe that transfusions of competent adults can be undertaken without significant risk. The patient who is transfused may feel condemned to eternal damnation and the publicity, often quite critical, that follows a forced transfusion can be widespread.

There are several reported negligence actions brought by surviving families after the death of patients from hemorrhage when the patients had refused transfusion. In one, *Shorter v. Drury*, Mrs. Shorter underwent a dilation and curettage procedure for a missed abortion. Prior to the procedure, both she and her husband signed a release form, a portion of which stated that "I hereby release the hospital, its personnel, and the attending physician from any responsibility whatever for unfavorable reactions or any untoward results due to my refusal to permit the use of blood or its derivatives and I fully understand the possible consequences of such refusal on my part."[12] About one hour after the procedure, Mrs. Shorter began to bleed heavily and went into shock. An exploratory laparotomy revealed that Dr. Drury had lacerated her uterus severely with the curette. As long as she was coherent, Mrs. Shorter refused to consent to transfusion. Thereafter, her husband also continued to refuse. She died of hemorrhage. The physicians involved agreed that her death would have been unlikely had transfusions been administered.

Mr. Shorter later brought a wrongful death action. He claimed that his wife's death was proximately caused by the negligence of Dr. Drury when he lacerated the uterus. Mr. Shorter did not claim that transfusions should have been administered over his wife's objections. The jury found that Dr. Drury had been negligent and awarded $412,000. The jury then determined that Mr. and Mrs. Shorter had knowingly assumed the risk of death from hemorrhage and attributed 75 percent of the fault to them. This reduced the damages to $103,000. After the judgment was final, both parties appealed. The appeals court held that the release form was valid and enforceable, but that it did not release the physician from all liability under any circumstances. Instead, it released him from liability for the death but not from the liability for his negligence (he did not appeal the jury's finding that he was negligent).

The court went on to state that the "Shorters could be found by the jury to have assumed the risk of death from an operation which had to be performed without blood transfusions and where blood could not be administered under any circumstances including where the doctor made what would otherwise have been a correctable surgical mistake. The risk of death from a failure to receive a transfusion to which the Shorters exposed themselves was created by, and must be allocated to, the Shorters themselves."[13] The judgment was affirmed. The dissenting judges would have stricken the damages reduction since they agreed with the plaintiff's argument that the Shorters had assumed the risk of death from bleeding from non-negligent causes, but had not assumed the risk of death from the physician's negligence.

In *Randolph v. City of New York*, different questions were raised. In that case, Mrs. Randolph, age 45, was to undergo her fourth cesarean section and a tubal ligation. She was 5 feet, 4 inches in height and weighed over 200 pounds, and she was anemic. She had informed her obstetrician that she was a member of Jehovah's Witnesses. She declined blood transfusion if it became indicated. Nevertheless, she was typed and cross-matched for two units that were sent to the operating room. After the baby girl was delivered at 11:43 A.M., it became clear that there was a placenta accreta. A cesarean hysterectomy was done. During that procedure, the bladder was lacerated and hemorrhage from that site was massive. Within 15 minutes of the delivery, the patient was estimated to have lost 2,000 cc, or 40 percent, of her blood volume. Volume expanders were used. By 12:30 P.M. the patient had lost 80 percent of her blood volume and the anesthesiologist had someone in the operating room call the corporation counsel's office. When that office gave permission, he began transfusion (at about 12:45 P.M.). Hemorrhage was not controlled until 1:00 P.M., and the patient had a cardiac arrest at 1:15 P.M. She was pronounced dead at 2:00 P.M.

The husband sued the surgeon, anesthesiologist, and his employer, the City of New York. Prior to trial, the surgeon settled with the plaintiff for $350,000. Trial proceeded against the anesthesiologist. The claims were that he should have transfused despite Mrs. Randolph's refusal and that, once transfusion had begun, it was done negligently (that is, he infused too little blood at too slow a rate). The jury found for plaintiffs and awarded $2.5 million. Fifty percent of this amount was attributable to the defendants. The plaintiff agreed to a reduction of damages to $1 million. The defense appealed. On appeal, the plaintiff conceded at oral argument (although he had argued the contrary at trial) that if the anesthesiologist had not undertaken to transfuse the patient at all, he would not have been liable since he was merely following her wishes. The court held that he was not required to ignore her religious beliefs to assure her children support, because there was a capable surviving parent. Since both the plaintiff's expert witness and Dr. Foster, the anesthesiologist, agreed that Mrs. Randolph's condition became irreversible at about 12:30 P.M., the appeals court found that there was no malpractice on Dr. Foster's part. The verdict was reversed.[14]

Risk Management

These cases demonstrate three general principles that can be used to manage risk. First, release forms signed by Jehovah's Witnesses patients can be useful. They will demonstrate that the patient gave the instructions. When backed up by other medical record documentation, they also can show that the patient was competent and knowing in the refusal. The release form will not prevent a lawsuit, nor will it insulate the health care provider from damages caused by negligence. For example, the physician may be liable for the bladder laceration in the *Randolph* case but not totally responsible for the death that could have been prevented with adequate transfusion. Second, it is useful to have the spouse sign the release form along with the patient, although the physician and hospital cannot compel the spouse to sign it. Not all spouses share their religious beliefs, but if they do that fact should be documented. Even a spouse who does not agree often will be useful in making clear how strongly the patient believes in the refusal of blood transfusion. Third, when a decision is made to start transfusion, it must be done competently and rapidly.

Most health care facility attorneys advise that court orders to transfuse adult, competent Jehovah's Witnesses are difficult to obtain, especially if the bleeding has not already occurred. If, as is often the case, there has been time prior to the serious bleeding to discuss religious beliefs, it will be difficult to convince a judge to ignore them. When a court order is requested to transfuse a competent adult, the judge may come to the hospital for a hearing in the patient's room or in a nearby conference room if the patient can be moved. If an order is issued and the patient still objects, it may be necessary to place the patient in restraints to transfuse safely.

Documents filed in court to request a transfusion order are public and, unless sealed, can be read by anyone and reported in the press. These practical implications of the process for obtaining and implementing a court order should be made clear to the health care staff and considered in the decision to seek a court order. When the staff intends to transfuse a patient to avert death regardless of her consent, has so informed the patient, and is willing to face any legal consequences of that action, a request for a court order may be inadvisable. If it is denied, the staff then may be transfusing in the face of an explicit judicial decision finding the patient competent to refuse transfusion. Such an action has serious legal and practical consequences for damages, and it may adversely influence how the local court system views the facility and its physicians.

Fears of conflicts where death can be the consequence have convinced some obstetricians to refuse to care for patients who would, under all circumstances, refuse blood transfusion. This policy, if it occurs in a private practice, is legal as long as the patient is advised of it early enough to seek care elsewhere. A physician can be liable for abandonment if he or she withdraws from the care of a patient in labor. Questions about blood transfusion and other possible conflicts between medical and religious philosophies should be asked early during the pregnancy.

Many physicians do not refuse to care for patients who would refuse blood, but they indicate their feelings to their patients. For example, a physician may tell a patient he or she will do everything possible to avoid transfusion, but when the alternative for the patient is death, the physician cannot guarantee his or her reaction. This explanation will not relieve a physician of liability for transfusion without consent, but it will be reasonable evidence that the patient understood (and accepted, if she remained in the practice) the ethical and religious views of the health care provider responsible for making the decisions. Some physicians decline to perform high-risk elective procedures on patients who would decline transfusion if indicated. It is unlikely that a state hospital and its personnel would be legally permitted to decline to care for certain classes of patients on the basis of their religious beliefs. However, this is not to say that the staff at a state facility could not decline to perform an elective coronary artery bypass graft if, in the surgeon's judgment, the surgery would be unreasonably unsafe because the patient declined transfusion.

Conflicts arise among hospital staff members as well as between physician and patient. The operating room is unique in the fact that two physicians of attending rank have responsibility for a patient—the surgeon and the anesthesiologist. Either may have strongly held beliefs that may include the inability to allow a patient to hemorrhage to death if that death is preventable. When a patient is adamant in his or her refusal of blood, the surgeon should consult the anesthesia staff in advance and make an effort to obtain an anesthesiologist who can agree with the treatment plan. If this cannot be done, the staff must come to some understanding about who will make transfusion decisions. It may be necessary, for example, for the surgeon to hang the blood if he or she assumes total responsibility for the decisions. Documentation of the repeated discussions between staff and patient must be placed in the medical record to show that the physician had a reasonable belief in the strength of the patient's convictions.

When an unconscious, bleeding patient arrives in the emergency room, transfusion may be started immediately even if relatives claim that the patient would refuse transfusion. Generally, decisions that could result in death for the patient must be made by the patient, rather than relatives, unless the patient is in an indisputable terminal condition.

As this discussion indicates, issues of refusal of blood transfusion can be complicated and difficult. They involve many concerns of medical care and legal liability. The risk management department of a hospital can be a resource in these situations.

REFUSAL OF CESAREAN SECTION

A recent study reported that court orders for cesarean sections have been sought in 11 states.[15] Several of these cases have been published in the medical or legal literature. They represent examples of complete breakdown of communication and trust between health care providers and patients. It probably is not a coincidence that all the women involved in these cases were being treated in a teaching hospital or were on public assistance.[16] These situations are among the most difficult faced by health care providers and facilities. Most doctors and nurses watch with great emotion as an electronic fetal monitor tracing drifts to zero and know they cannot take any action.

Some commentators have stated that if a physician were to "diagnose a pregnant woman's medical condition properly, to inform her accurately and completely of the risks and benefits of refusal and acceptance of the recommended treatment (including that of fetal harm or demise), and to make a reasonable assessment of her mental capacity, he or she should not be subject to any legal liability for honoring the woman's refusal of treatment."[17] Many physicians, including those aware of the professional liability decisions in blood transfusion cases and those aware that a parent cannot sign a release as to the rights of a fetus after birth,[18] do not view the legal situation with the same equanimity. Still, many physicians and nurses believe that a competent pregnant woman should be able to refuse cesarean section. A recent committee opinion published by the American College of Obstetricians and Gynecologists noted as a conclusion that:

Obstetricians should refrain from performing procedures that are unwanted by a pregnant woman. The use of judicial authority to implement treatment regimens in order to protect the fetus violates the pregnant woman's autonomy. Furthermore, inappropriate reliance on judicial authority may lead to undesirable societal consequences, such as the criminalization of noncompliance with medical recommendations."[19]

Only one case involving refusal of cesarean section has reached the highest court in a state: *Jefferson v. Griffin Spalding County Hospital Authority*.[20] Jessie Mae Jefferson was 39 weeks pregnant and was diagnosed as having a complete placenta previa. She refused cesarean section despite information about her likelihood of survival and that of the baby in the event of vaginal delivery. She and her husband refused the surgery and any associated blood transfusion on the basis of religious beliefs. The county hospital authority sought a court order to compel the patient to undergo the surgery prior to the onset of labor. The court refused this request but granted the request to approve the surgery in the event the patient presented herself to the hospital for delivery. The court suggested that it would reconsider its ruling if an appropriate state agency made a request.

The next day the Georgia Department of Human Resources, which was charged with the care of abused and neglected children, petitioned the court to have the fetus declared neglected under state law (state law in most states defines neglect, in part, as the failure of parents to provide medically necessary treatment). The court concluded that the child was viable and was entitled to the protection of the Georgia Juvenile Code. It therefore granted temporary custody of the child to the State of Georgia Department of Human Resources with authority to consent to the cesarean section. The custody was to terminate at the birth or death of the child, whichever came first. An appeal followed. The Supreme Court of Georgia denied a stay and affirmed the lower court decision. Mrs. Jefferson delivered a healthy baby without surgery a few days later.[21]

Other cases have involved patients in labor when there was considerably less time than there was in the *Jefferson* case. In one a 33-year-old woman with no prenatal care was admitted at 7:30 A.M. She was morbidly obese and her pregnancy had not been recognized during a cholecystectomy and a re-exploration of the common bile duct, both of which had been performed during pregnancy. Her membranes had ruptured two hours prior to admission and fluid was clear. She was 2 cm dilated. By 9:00 A.M., she was 3 cm dilated and the amniotic fluid was meconium-stained. The patient asked to leave against medical advice but relented after persuasion. At 11:00 A.M. late decelerations appeared on the fetal heart rate tracing. At noon the patient refused recommended cesarean section. A psychiatrist evaluated the patient between 1:00 P.M. and 2:00 P.M. and found her neither delusional nor incompetent. Late decelerations and decreased heart rate variability persisted. The patient's relatives tried and failed to persuade her to consent to the cesarean section. At 5:00 P.M., the judge and attorneys representing the mother and fetus arrived, and a hearing was conducted. The judge ordered the surgery, and it was performed at about 6:30 P.M. The infant had Apgars of 2 and 8 with a cord pH of 7.20. The infant experienced transient respiratory distress attributable to intrapartal asphyxia but then did well. The mother did well except for delayed healing of the upper portion of the incision.[22]

While such cases are, thankfully, uncommon, they continue to occur. In an ongoing case, the District of Columbia Court of Appeals is considering the case of Angela Carder, who was in the 25th week of gestation when she was diagnosed as having terminal lung cancer. On June 16, 1987, the patient's condition was worsening; the fetus was then 26 weeks' gestation.

Although the medical staff had agreed on passive treatment since the mother was terminal and the baby's chances of survival were also grim, the hospital filed an action in the superior court to seek authority to perform a cesarean section. A hearing was held that day, but Mrs. Carder was sedated and could not give her opinion. Her husband refused cesarean section, and there was conflicting testimony about what Mrs. Carder would have wanted. The court found that the fetus was viable and ordered the surgery. On the same day, the trial court's order was appealed to the District of Columbia Court of Appeals, which denied the requested stay of the order.[23] The cesarean section was performed. The infant died shortly after the surgery, and the mother died two days later.

A petition for rehearing was filed after Mrs. Carder's death. The court of appeals agreed to hear the case because of its importance. The decision has not been rendered.

Risk Management

The best risk management in cesarean section refusal cases is prevention. Every effort should be made to maintain an acceptable relationship with the patient by using whatever personnel are available: the attending physician, a social worker, a minister, family members, a family physician, or anyone the patient trusts. While some physicians may consider blood transfusion without patient consent, it is unlikely that any would consider performing a cesarean section without patient consent or a court order. Family consent could be acceptable if the patient were to be judged incompetent. The process of obtaining a court order can take some hours. The judge may then refuse to appoint a guardian to consent to the surgery, and the staff will be forced to accept the patient's decision. Nevertheless, it has been reported that health care providers were successful in obtaining court orders in 86 percent of the cases in which an order was sought.[24] In 47 percent of these cases the diagnosis was fetal distress.[25] None of these patients was considered incompetent by a psychiatrist, although all were evaluated.[26]

SUMMARY

The American College of Obstetricians and Gynecologists concludes that "every reasonable effort should be made to protect the fetus, but the pregnant woman's autonomy should be respected."[27] It also states, "The use of the courts to resolve these conflicts is almost never warranted."[28] Nevertheless, the staff should feel free to call a consultant from an institutional ethics committee or other colleagues for support in making the decision that appears correct under the circumstances. The case circumstances and decision must be carefully documented and, preferably, include rationale.

NOTES

1. American College of Obstetricians and Gynecologists, "Prevention of RHO(D) Isoimmunization," *American College of Obstetricians and Gynecologists Technical Bulletin No. 79* (August 1984); See also, *Technical Bulletin No. 90.*

2. *Truman v. Thomas,* 611 P.2d 902 (Cal. 1980), 905.

3. *Taft v. Taft,* 446 N.E.2d 395 (Mass. 1983).

4. D. Sacks and R. Koppes, "Blood Transfusion and Jehovah's Witnesses: Medical and Legal Issues in Obstetrics and Gynecology," *American Journal of Obstetrics and Gynecology* 154 (1986): 483.

5. A. Holder, "Parents, Courts and Refusal of Treatment," *Journal of Pediatrics* 103 (1983): 515.

6. *Walker v. Superior Court,* 253 Cal. Rptr. 1 (Cal. 1988).

7. *Crouse Irving Memorial Hospital, Inc. v. Paddock,* 485 N.Y.S.2d 443 (Sup. 1985).

8. Ibid., 445.

9. Ibid., 446.

10. *Mercy Hospital, Inc. v. Jackson,* 489 A.2d 1130 (Md. App. 1985), 1134.

11. *Malette v. Shulman,* 63 O.R.(2d) 243 (December 21, 1987).

12. *Shorter v. Drury,* 695 P.2d 116 (Wash. 1985), 119.

13. Ibid., 123.

14. *Randolph v. City of New York,* 501 N.Y.S.2d 837 (A.D. 1 Dept. 1986).

15. V. Kolder et al., "Court-Ordered Obstetrical Interventions," *New England Journal of Medicine* 316 (1987): 1192.

16. Ibid. See also J. Daniels, "Court-Ordered Cesareans: A Growing Concern for Indigent Women," *Clearinghouse Review* (February 1988): 1064.

17. L. Nelson and N. Milliken, "Compelled Medical Treatment of Pregnant Women: Life, Liberty, and Law in Conflict," *Journal of the American Medical Association* 259 (1988): 1060.

18. See A. Holder, *Legal Issues in Pediatrics and Adolescent Medicine,* 2d ed. (New Haven: Yale University Press, 1985), 160.

19. American College of Obstetricians and Gynecologists: Committee on Ethics, "Patient Choice: Maternal-Fetal Conflict," No. 55 (October 1987).

20. *Jefferson v. Griffin Spalding County Hospital Authority,* 274 S.E.2d 457 (Ga. 1981).

21. G. Annas, "Forced Cesareans: The Most Unkindest Cut of All," *Hastings Center Report* 12 (1982): 16.

22. W. Bowes and B. Selgestad, "Fetal versus Maternal Rights: Medical and Legal Perspectives," *Obstetrics and Gynecology* 58 (1981): 209.

23. *In Re A.C.*, 533 A.2d 611 (D.C. App. 1987).

24. Kolder, "Court-Ordered Obstetrical Interventions," 1193.

25. Ibid.

26. Ibid., 1195.

27. American College of Obstetricians and Gynecologists: Committee on Ethics, "Patient Choice," 2.

28. Ibid.

SUGGESTED READINGS

Field, D. et al. 1988. Maternal brain death during pregnancy: Medical and ethical issues. *Journal of the American Medical Association* 260:816.

Finamore, E. 1983. Jefferson v. Griffin Spaulding County Hospital Authority: Court-ordered surgery to protect the life of an unborn child. *American Journal of Law & Medicine* 9:83.

Holder, A. 1985. Maternal-fetal conflicts and the law. *The Female Patient* 10 (June): 80.

Jost, K. 1989. Mother versus child. *American Bar Association Journal* (April): 84.

Loewy, E. 1987. The pregnant brain dead and the fetus: Must we always try to wrest life from death? *American Journal of Obstetrics and Gynecology* 157:1097.

Remick, D. 1988. Whose life is it anyway? *Washington Post Magazine* (February 21): 14.

Rhoden, N. 1986. The judge in the delivery room: The emergence of court-ordered cesareans. *California Law Review* 74:1951.

Rhoden, N. 1987. Cesareans and samaritans. *Law, Medicine and Health Care* 15:118.

Rhoden, N. 1987. Informed consent in obstetrics: Some special problems. *Western New England Law Review* 9:67.

Shrader, D. 1986. On dying more than one death. *Hastings Center Report* 16 (February): 12.

Chapter 10

Routine Professional
Liability Risks

10

Risks occur in any hospital or office practice. Many are not unique to obstetrical practice but can occur under slightly different circumstances in other practice specialty areas. Some risks may seem small, but even a small incident can seriously injure a patient or a staff member.

MEDICATION ERRORS

Most nurses and other health care professionals know that medication errors can occur frequently. In 1985 St. Paul Fire and Marine Insurance Company, a professional liability insurance carrier, reported data on medication claims against physicians and hospitals. Table 10–1 includes data on more than 1,800 claims involving physicians. The company noted that the number of drug-related claims against physicians rose 78 percent between 1979 and August 1985 with costs up 168 percent. Claims related to drug side effects rose 156 percent during that period, with costs up 143 percent.[1]

Table 10–2 reports on 752 hospital medication claims between May 1982 and August 1985. These claims constituted 6.5 percent of the carrier's total hospital claims and accounted for 5.9 percent of the total

---

Table 10–1   Physician Medication Claims, St. Paul Fire and Marine Insurance
Company

St. Paul Fire and Marine Drug-Related Claims
Physicians
Reported 1979–August 1985

Allegation	No. of Claims	% of Claims	Average Cost*
Improper treatment—drug side effect	898	47.5%	$32,683
Improper treatment—drug incorrect	437	23.1	23,762
Improper treatment—drug overdose	262	13.9	26,153
Failure to diagnose—drug-related problems	99	5.2	27,702
Improper treatment—prescription incorrect	99	5.2	18,126
Improper treatment—drug addiction	96	5.1	30,466
Total Drug-Related Allegations	1,891	100%	$28,581

*Average cost includes total amount paid and reserved plus allocated legal expenses.

Source: Reprinted from *Malpractice Digest*, Vol. 12, No. 3, with permission of St. Paul Fire and Marine Insurance Company, © Fall 1985.

---

incurred cost. Nurses were involved in 46 percent of the claims, and physicians were involved in 28 percent.[2]

Medication errors have occurred in every aspect of medication administration. Incorrect medications have been administered, incorrect routes used, and incorrect doses or concentrations of medications mixed and used. At times, the wrong patient has been medicated. The correct patient may have been medicated at the wrong time because of an incorrect dose schedule. Two doses have been given the same patient at the correct time by two different nurses, because the first nurse had not charted the first dose before the second dose was given. Patients also have been medicated with the correct doses but unacceptably early or late (defined as a medication error by many hospital policies when medication is given outside the permissible time period).

A medication error is often a violation of a standard of care. Often, there is no credible argument that the harm suffered from the error could

Table 10–2   Hospital Medication Claims, St. Paul Fire and Marine Insurance Company

St. Paul Fire and Marine Drug-Related Claims
Hospitals
Reported May 1982–August 1985

Hospital Location or Service	No. of Claims	% of Claims	Average Cost*
Nursing or patient care areas	413	54.9%	$18,335
Emergency services	100	13.3	20,243
Surgical services	81	10.8	30,424
Labor/delivery/nursery	48	6.4	19,790
Outpatient surgery	24	3.2	10,495
Psychiatric services	18	2.4	10,806
Other hospital locations	68	9.0	4,174
All Hospital Locations	752	100%	$18,273

Allegation	No. of Claims	% of Claims	Average Cost*
Wrong amount or rate	179	23.8%	$17,292
Undesired result of medication	169	22.5	18,279
Wrong medication given	160	21.3	14,561
Improper route of administration	80	10.6	27,023
Omitted or delayed medication	28	3.7	11,550
Other medication issues	136	18.1	20,159
Total Medication-Related Allegations	752	100%	$18,273

*Average cost includes total amount paid and reserved plus allocated legal expenses.

Source: Reprinted from *Malpractice Digest*, Vol. 12, No. 3, with permission of St. Paul Fire and Marine Insurance Company, © Fall 1985.

have occurred if due care had been exercised. A case sometimes can be defended by arguing causation or damages. For example, a medication error may have occurred but be unrelated to the patient's unfortunate outcome, or it may have caused no damage to the patient (or her fetus). Because medication errors often are examples of clear liability, claims are frequently settled prior to trial. If a medication error case does go to trial, it is possible for the defendants to admit liability and to try the case for a determination of damages only. This strategy may help the defendants by eliminating testimony of the individuals responsible for the error and focusing on the main defense argument in the case.

An older case illustrates some of the problems in actions involving medication errors. A child, Robyn Norton, was born in September 1959. Congenital heart disease was diagnosed in early December. She was admitted on December 15, 1959, for further evaluation required prior to heart surgery. An order was written for "Elixir Pediatric Lanoxin 2.5 cc (0.125 mg) q6h X 3 then once daily." Although this order contained no route of administration, the Lanoxin was administered orally as intended. The child was discharged on December 16. She was readmitted on December 29 when her condition worsened. On January 2, 1960, the physician examined the infant and ordered "3.0 cc Lanoxin today for one dose only." A nursing supervisor, although concerned that 3 cc was a large dose, was not aware that the medication came in a form for oral administration, nor did she inquire of other staff, pharmacy personnel, or the attending physician. She administered the 3 cc in a divided intramuscular dose to the baby, who died of the overdose 75 minutes later.

The family sued the doctor, nurse, and hospital for the death of the child. It was conceded at trial that 3 cc of the elixir was a therapeutic dose, but 3 cc of the injectable form was a lethal overdose. Judgment was rendered for the parents (for about $23,000) and the defendants appealed. The court held that the physician was liable for his failure to note the route of administration and that the nurse and the hospital, as her employer, were liable for the failure of the nurse to question the prescribed dose and route when she was not familiar enough with the medication. The judgment was reduced to $10,000.[3]

A medication error is a classic mistake that occurs because a physician, nurse, pharmacist, or other staff member is inattentive or uninformed. For example, there is no substitute or excuse for failing to be familiar with a medication and for failing to read a label on a medication bottle before drawing up the substance. The patient's medical record should reflect the medication error if it is known, and the patient or the family should be told the truth about the situation, especially if the patient has deteriorated clinically. However, the staff should not speculate to the patient if the cause of the patient's deterioration is not clearly related to the error. Laboratory values may be needed before the staff assumes, or the family is told, for instance, that the patient's arrhythmias were caused by a potassium medication error.

Some medication errors can be prevented by changes in substance packaging. It is common for multiple dose vials of potassium chloride and sodium chloride, for example, to be stored together. Both substances are clear liquids and can be purchased in identical bottles. If a staff member does not read the label on a particular vial, a serious medication error may occur. Health care facilities can minimize this possibility by purchasing the solutions in nonidentical bottles, or in other cases, by arranging for a harmless coloring to be placed in one solution (as in isopropyl alcohol on scrub tables in the operating room). Different packaging may cost the facility slightly more but may prevent one or more significant instances of patient harm.

The facility also must be attentive to supplier-generated changes in packaging that may confuse the staff. Errors are more common when a color-coded flip top on a vial is changed to the same color as one on another commonly used vial. This type of error reflects the fact that the staff does sometimes rely on visual cues in lieu of reading labels.

Other medication problems and errors can be prevented when physicians, nurses, and pharmacists cooperate in the exercise of due care. Physicians should avoid giving verbal orders, because they can be heard incorrectly and then transcribed incorrectly. To minimize errors, the nurse receiving a verbal order should transcribe it with care and repeat it back to the ordering physician. Written orders should be legible. If a prescription or order is illegible, the nurse or pharmacist must call the prescribing physician to verify the information. A prescription for Ritadrine for premature labor can cause harm when the pharmacist fills it with Ritalin after misreading the handwriting. Abbreviations should be used with care. "Q.D." can be mistaken for "O.D." (the abbreviation for the right eye), and medications intended for oral use may be applied to the eye. Every order should include the dose, route of administration, frequency of administration, and other pertinent information. If a nurse believes that medication is improperly prescribed, the nurse has an independent duty of care to confirm the order. A nurse may refuse to administer a medication that appears to be an overdose, for example, but when she does this she must notify the prescribing physician so that a new order can be given.

Medications prescribed at discharge or in the office should be documented by dose, frequency of administration, and number of days of medication prescribed. An office note stating only that ampicillin was prescribed is insufficient. Every prescribing practitioner should make it a practice to discuss any foreseeable side effects with a patient, particularly if there may be fetal effects.

Even the arguably correct administration of medications can cause other patient problems upon which a claim may be made. Typically, these are cases in which personnel are not clearly liable. In *Tripp v. Humana, Inc.*, Marilyn Tripp was hospitalized for the delivery of her baby. During the hospitalization the patient received three injections, one in each thigh and one in her hip. On the day of discharge the patient apparently noticed a red spot at the site of each injection. During the subsequent two weeks, the patient developed increasing redness at the injection sites, a fever that eventually reached 104° F., and stiffness and soreness in her legs. She was admitted to another hospital where she was treated for gangrene in her arms and legs. Her treatment included the surgical removal of affected tissues and plastic surgery.

She sued the first hospital, its corporate owner, a nurse, and a physician (who was later dropped from the suit). She claimed that the nurse failed to assure the sterility of the syringe, needle, and medication and that the injection technique was inadequate. The Supreme Court of Alabama found material facts in dispute and remanded the case for trial.[4] The opinion does not indicate the final outcome of the case (whether it was settled or tried).

Finally, medication-related claims also include instances in which it is alleged that the health care provider failed to monitor drug therapy or failed to prescribe an appropriate medication. As an example of the latter, consider the following facts. In June 1983 a case of a 35-year-old woman was reported. She was two months pregnant and was hospitalized for deep vein iliofemoral thrombophlebitis of the left leg from groin to ankle. She was treated with bed rest and elevation of the leg, but heparin was not prescribed. The patient underwent therapeutic abortion seven days later without anticoagulation therapy. She died two days later of multiple pulmonary emboli. The lawsuit claimed that the physician was negligent when he failed to prescribe heparin, which does not cross the placenta and can be prescribed for pregnant women when indicated. The case was settled for $475,000.[5]

RETAINED FOREIGN BODIES

Foreign bodies are occasionally left inside surgical patients inadvertently. Prosthetic devices and other objects may be left there intentionally as part of the procedure. Many surgical facilities subject some surgical equipment, such as sponges, needles, sharps, and surgical instruments, to one or more counts during procedures. These items can be easily left inside patients. Also a portion of an instrument, needle, or catheter may break off during a procedure but go unnoticed by operating room personnel. Depending on the circumstances, retrieval of the retained foreign body may take place at a later surgery, or it may be left inside the patient if it will do no harm or less harm than a second surgical procedure.

A case that involves a retained sponge is difficult to defend. Other cases may be less clear. Some of them may relate to malfunctions and other problems with medical devices and involve product liability law. In obstetrical cases, sponges have been retained within the abdomen during cesarean section or postpartum tubal ligations. They also have been left for days in the vagina, where they can cause cervical and vaginal wall erosions and contribute to episiotomy infections. During surgical cases, it is the joint responsibility of the physicians and nursing staff to ensure that foreign materials are not inadvertently left in the patient. Sponges are not usually counted during deliveries. It remains the responsibility of the physician or nurse-midwife doing the delivery to check the vagina for retained sponges after any tissue repair is completed.

PATIENT BURNS AND FALLS

Patients are periodically burned by devices such as hot water bottles, physical therapy treatments, casting materials, or grounding pads. If the patient is under anesthesia, medicated, or even intoxicated, the staff has responsibility for preventing most foreseeable burns. Care should be taken to prevent burns and when they do occur to treat the injuries promptly to minimize any disability and scarring.

Many patients who sustain falls in hospitals are elderly, but some are not. A recent study showed that about half of the alert patients who had falls in a hospital fell from bed; another 25 percent fell while trying to get to the bathroom.[6] On obstetrical and postpartum units, patients may fall when they become dizzy upon arising, or they may trip over an IV pole. Not all of these falls can be prevented, but proper education of patients will reduce the number. Patients should be taught how to arise from bed or a chair to minimize orthostatic hypotension. Generally, patients who have been sedated should remain in bed with the side rails up (despite the fact that some patients climb over the rails). A physician may order that side rails be kept up, but in most hospitals a nurse may also make that judgment without a physician's order. As a practical matter, it may be impossible in this type of situation for a nurse to defend a case involving a patient's fall by showing that the physician did not order the rails to be raised at all times.

Babies also fall in hospitals. Typically, these falls occur when babies are placed on beds or counters and left unattended for a moment. Some falls occur when a mother is alone with her child. These falls may not be reported to the staff.

It is worthwhile for the staff to develop an educational sheet for new admissions to the postpartum floor. This device orients the mother to the floor and its rules about visiting, siblings, and privacy and can begin the process of educating a new mother about the care of an infant. Since infant falls also occur at home, it is not too early to teach mothers how to prevent them. The patient's receipt of these educational materials should be documented.

ANESTHESIA

Patients of any gestation may have occasion to receive regional or general anesthesia for a surgical procedure. Some anesthesiologists and hospitals continue to use a single consent form for anesthesia and surgery, but others now use separate forms. With a single form, the attending surgeon, who is not an anesthesia expert, may be or at least feel legally responsible for ensuring that the patient accepts the risk of anesthesia. A hospital may resist the use of two forms, because it wishes to discourage the proliferation of separate consent forms in general. The solution to the question of forms involves policy and politics. From a legal perspective, either approach can be adequate as long as the medical record documents the contents of discussions with the patient by both the anesthesiologist and the attending surgeon and clearly indicates that consent has been obtained. If a patient limits consent, this fact should be noted and discussed with the staff. (See Chapter 9 concerning refusal of blood during surgery.)

In the past many patients delivered vaginally under general anesthesia, but now most patients deliver under local anesthesia or a form of regional anesthesia. Anesthesiologists are at a disadvantage when they must inform a patient in active labor, who is anxious for pain relief, about the risk of regional anesthesia. Some anesthesia groups have developed patient education sheets in collaboration with local obstetricians. These can be distributed to interested patients in obstetrical practices, clinics, and childbirth classes. The patient obstetrical record should reflect that the patient has received these (and other) educational materials and that all questions have been answered. The use of informational material does not create a presumption that the patient possessed enough information to give consent, but it does assist the physician to show that the patient knew of any risks.

Regional anesthesia claims during obstetrics generally fall into two categories: (1) problems with the anesthesia, such as an inadvertent spinal during epidural administration that results in a spinal headache or in a very high level of anesthesia, and (2) hypotension that results in fetal distress. These complications can occur in the absence of negligence; that is, they can be a risk of the procedure even when it is properly performed. Since it is unlikely that a patient could show that an epidural resulting in a recognized inadvertent spinal tap, for example, was improperly performed, the claims tend to include informed consent allegations. Sometimes, anesthesia and obstetrical claims are combined as, for example, in a case of delayed recognition of epidural-related hypotension with fetal distress.

The Risk Management Foundation of the Harvard Medical Institutions recently published a study of 36 anesthesia claims that occurred between April 1976 and December 1984. These claims resulted in total losses of $4,581,704. Two actions involved obstetrics: (1) a patient claimed an inadequate spinal anesthesia under which a cesarean section was performed (she claimed pain and psychological damage) and (2) a delivery was witnessed by drug company representatives invited to the hospital by the anesthesia department (allegedly without the mother's consent). In general, the study found that claims of improper administration of anesthesia, while not the most common claims, were by far the most expensive in terms of losses.[7]

INFECTION

Infections contracted in a hospital may be unpreventable, but exposure to certain infections is preventable. Since the human immunodeficiency virus (HIV) and hepatitis virus, among others, can be transmitted via needle sticks, hospital and office staffs must use universal precautions as recommended by the Centers for Disease Control (CDC).[8] The failure to follow these recommendations or the failure to dispose of blood-contaminated sharps carefully can expose both staff members and patients to infection risk and result in subsequent legal actions. Many hospitals have provided boxes near patients to facilitate disposal of used hypodermic syringes and scalpels so that recapping, the most common cause of needle-stick injuries to staff, occurs less often. Staff members should not leave used needles on patient tables, trays, chair arms, or other convenient spots. Patients and visitors have sat on needles left on chairs and stepped on needles dropped on the floor (the patient is often wearing paper slippers). Visiting children have picked up needles left from patients and played with them. All of these exposures are preventable. It is likely that a jury would find a hospital and its employees liable for patient or visitor injuries sustained as a result of careless disposal of potentially infectious materials.

If patients or visitors are exposed via contaminated needles to infection risk, the hospital should offer the kind of testing provided for its employees when they are exposed. This usually includes HIV and hepatitis testing. The staff often knows which patient's blood contaminated the needle in question. If the HIV or hepatitis status of that patient is known to be positive, the exposed employee or patient may be more concerned about a risk of seroconversion. However, even an HIV negative patient can be infectious. When the patient's status is not known, the staff or attending physician can ask the source patient to be tested. The patient may decline. If there is no statute permitting testing without consent under these circumstances, there is little likelihood that the patient can be forced to undergo testing.

Legislatures have been concerned about health care providers, law enforcement authorities, and others who are exposed to blood and body fluids and who are unable to determine the HIV status of the exposure source. Legislation is pending in several states that could permit HIV testing without consent, but the usefulness of these statutes varies with their wording. For example, Connecticut recently passed a law that permits HIV testing of a source patient without consent only if the following five conditions are met:

1. The health care worker must have been exposed to an HIV infection during the performance of work, report the exposure within 48 hours, and include details of the incident, and the exposure must pose a "significant risk" of transmission to the worker, as defined in forthcoming regulations.
2. The worker must submit to HIV testing within 72 hours of the occupational exposure, and be negative on the test.
3. The source patient, if living, must be asked for his or her consent to voluntary testing, and must refuse.
4. The risk must be certified as significant in writing by a group of three impartial health care providers.
5. The worker must be able to take meaningful action (as defined by the regulation) based on the test, which action "could not otherwise be taken."[9]

Employee Infection Control Requirements

Hepatitis, HIV, and other diseases have been transmitted in the health care environment. The CDC reported in September 1988 that about 5 percent of all adults known to have acquired immunodeficiency syndrome (AIDS), for whom occupational data were available, were employed in health care settings. Most of these workers reported risk factors for the disease, but the mode of acquisition of the virus was unknown for 169 of them. Additional data were available for 44 of these workers: 8 were physicians (including 4 surgeons); 1 was a dentist; 6 were nurses; 9, nursing assistants; 8, housekeeping or maintenance workers; 2, respiratory therapists; 4, clinical laboratory technicians; 1 was a paramedic; and 1 was an embalmer. The remaining 4 workers reported no patient contact.[10]

The CDC has published infection control recommendations for both routine and invasive work. Universal precautions are recommended for work with tissue and cerebrospinal, pleural, synovial, peritoneal, pericardial, and amniotic fluids. These precautions apply to blood, semen, vaginal secretions, and other body fluids that contain visible blood. They do not apply to feces, nasal secretions, sputum, sweat, tears, urine, and vomitus unless they contain visible blood.[11] The CDC recommendations are considered minimal. Many hospitals have chosen to retain a broader definition of at-risk body fluids, especially in areas where the incidence of patient exposure to the human immunodeficiency or hepatitis virus is relatively high.

Employers are required by federal law to provide safe workplaces for employees. The Occupational Safety and Health Administration (OSHA) inspects health care facilities for compliance. Health care employers must classify the tasks performed by employees and document that appropriate universal precaution training has occurred. Failure by an employer to protect its employees may subject the employer to a fine of up to $10,000 per incident (for which insurance is not available). A fine may be imposed even if an employee, as a professional matter, declines to use offered and available protective equipment. These rules also may be applied to most private practices, since they are also employers.

Health care facilities have become much more attentive to employee safety practices. They must enforce infection control rules through employee discipline, if necessary. Hospitals have also chosen to require their nonemployed medical and professional staffs to comply with institutional infection control rules or risk withdrawal of hospital privileges.

KIDNAPPING

Several times a year children, often infants, are kidnapped from hospitals. The kidnappers may be hospital volunteers or employees, strangers, or family members. Most often these children are found, but in some cases it takes weeks or months. Some children are never found. A hospital owes its patients a duty to check credentials of staff members (to a varying degree, depending upon the proposed function of each staff member) and owes a duty to provide general supervision and security. There is, unfortunately, no way to predict which of the many persons who may properly enter a hospital are prospective kidnappers. Therefore, the staff must be vigilant about persons who appear near the nursery without reason. Mothers must be told not to leave their babies alone in their rooms when they plan to bathe or be absent from the room for other reasons. The staff must continually check on the location of the babies. All of this attention may not prevent a kidnapping, and even if one is prevented, the fact of its deterrence will not be known to the staff. Precautions may seem tiresome and unrewarding, but they are very necessary and should be maintained. Clippings about kidnappings from other hospitals periodically posted on the staff bulletin board may be sufficient to keep the staff motivated.

When a kidnapper is caught, criminal charges are brought by local or federal authorities. The family also may sue the facility from which the child was removed, whether or not the police have recovered the baby. Claims of this kind, several of which are currently pending, are for parental emotional distress caused by allegedly negligent personnel evaluation and security services.

VERBAL ORDERS

Most hospitals permit practitioners to order medications and patient treatments verbally, either in person or over the telephone. When the verbal order is received it should be repeated to the prescribing practitioner for verification. Usually, verbal orders also must be cosigned by the ordering practitioner within a reasonable period of time. Verbal orders should be treated with caution, especially if they are vague. For example, a physician could verbally (or in writing) order "insulin as per patient's home schedule." This requires that the nurse check with the patient and also assumes that the patient is attentive and mentally capable of accurately telling the nurse about the usual insulin routine. If there is any question about the nurse's ability to get an accurate description from the patient or close family, the nurse should take the results of that discussion and reconfirm the order with the physician before administering an important medication.

Orders for some medications or for some important area of care, such as do-not-resuscitate orders, may not be received as verbal orders according to hospital policy. These rules are not required by law, but a hospital staff may create and enforce rules that are much more rigorous than the law requires. In hospitals where strict policies have been created to avoid errors, a professional liability action may be difficult to defend if a policy is not followed and the foreseeable error results. In other cases, policies are used as guidelines when staff members occasionally fail to follow a hospital rule for what seemed at the time to be a good clinical reason.

SHORT STAFFING

For the past two years, there has been a nursing shortage of substantial proportions. The end of that shortage is not yet in sight. Even without a national shortage, there are always days or shifts when nurses may be scarce because of vacations, illness, or personnel needs of other floors.

A hospital has obligations under state licensure law and under accreditation rules to provide adequate staff for the patients (at their acuity) who are admitted. If the hospital cannot or does not do this and patient harm results, the hospital, as a corporate entity, may be liable. The nursing staff must be sure to notify nursing administration when extra staff is needed, even though there may be no staff to send to the floor. The nurse's responsibility, however, does not end here. The patients must be cared for by staff that is available. The charge nurse must consider the patient/ nurse assignment with care to ensure that the skills of the staff are appropriately used. It may be necessary to set priorities to determine those treatments that can be given, and those that cannot. For example, medications must be given, but the babies may not get their baths on that particular shift.

A case from New York illustrates this point. A patient with pneumonitis was admitted. He was febrile, lacked coordination, and had blurred vision. He was placed in a private room with a balcony that had a rail two to three feet high. After admission, the patient was seen on the balcony by nearby construction workers who called hospital personnel. The nursing staff had not noticed him on the balcony. A nurse returned the patient to his room and placed him in a posey restraint. She then called the doctor who ordered the staff to watch the patient. The staff was busy and there was no one available to stay with the patient, so the nurse called the patient's wife at her job. The wife could not come but promised to send her mother; she asked that the patient be watched until her mother got there (estimated to be about ten minutes). The nurse replied that she did not have the staff even for this, although the evidence showed that a practical nurse had been sent to supper during this ten-minute period. The patient escaped from the posey and fell from the balcony before his mother-in-law arrived.

In the lawsuit that followed, there was a plaintiff's judgment for both short staffing and the failure of the staff to set priorities for the short period of time until a family member could arrive. As the court made clear, the staff has the right of a meal break during a shift. However, the staff may have a conflicting duty to the patient, and a ten-minute delay in a meal break is not unreasonable to prevent a possible and foreseeable harm.

Where staffing is short, most commentators do not recommend that the nurse, physical therapist, or other staff member note in a patient's chart that staff was short and that was why a particular treatment was omitted. The omission of the treatment will be clear from the chart in any case. The attribution of the omission to short staffing as a sole cause may raise a question of inadequate treatment that would be unjustified under the circumstances.

SUMMARY

There are many examples of staff conduct that can result in preventable patient injury. Some of these are discussed in other chapters addressing specific aspects of obstetrical care. Common errors, such as those involving medication, occur in all patient care facilities and private practice offices. They occur because staff members are busy and are distracted from the task at hand. Errors have the potential to be quite serious, although fortunately most are minor and result in no actual harm to patients. Every effort should be made to prevent the occurrence of common and foreseeable errors.

NOTES

1. St. Paul Fire and Marine Insurance Company, "Medication-Related Claims on the Rise," *Malpractice Digest* 12 (Fall 1985): 3.

2. Ibid.

3. *Norton v. Argonaut Insurance Company*, 144 So.2d 249 (Ct. App. La. 1962).

4. *Tripp v. Humana, Inc.*, 474 So.2d 88 (Ala. 1985).

5. *Filardi v. Salter*, cited in *Malpractice Digest*, 1.

6. A. Halpert and J. Connors, "Prevention of Patient Falls through Perceived Control and Other Techniques," *Law, Medicine & Health Care* 14 (1986): 20.

7. E. Bowyer, "Anesthesia Claims Study Identifies Recurring Areas of Loss," *Risk Management Foundation Forum* 7 (1986): 14.

208   MALPRACTICE IN CLINICAL OBSTETRICAL NURSING

8. Occupational Safety and Health Administration, U.S. Department of Labor, "Occupational Exposure to Bloodborne Pathogens," *Federal Register* 54 (1989): 23042–138.

9. *Conn. Public Act.* 89–246 (1989).

10. U.S. Public Health Service, Centers for Disease Control, *Guidelines for Prevention of Transmission of Human Immunodeficiency Virus and Hepatitis B Virus to Health-Care and Public-Safety Workers: A Response to P.L. 100–607* (Atlanta, Ga.: CDC, February 1989), 4.

11. U.S. Public Health Service, Centers for Disease Control, "Update: Universal Precautions for Prevention of Transmission of Human Immunodeficiency Virus, Hepatitis B Virus, and Other Bloodborne Pathogens in Health Care Settings," *Morbidity and Mortality Weekly Report* 37 (1988): 377.

SUGGESTED READINGS

Allan, E., and K. Barker. 1990. Fundamentals of medication error research. *American Journal of Hospital Pharmacy* 47:555.

Brown, G. 1979. Medication errors: A case study. *Hospitals* (October 16): 61.

Creighton, H. 1986. Understaffing, Part 1. *Nursing Management* 17 (April): 24.

Creighton, H. 1986. Understaffing, Part 2. *Nursing Management* 17 (May): 14.

Hill, B., R. Johnson, and B. Garrett. 1988. Reducing the incidence of falls in high risk patients. *Journal of Nursing Administration* 18 (July/August): 24.

Koska, M. 1989. Drug errors: Dangerous, costly and avoidable. *Hospitals* (June 5): 24.

Chapter 11

Risk Management
Techniques in
Offices and Hospitals

11

Risk management techniques have been widely adopted by health care facilities and individuals in practice during the past few years. These techniques include education in methods of medical record documentation, attention to details of this documentation, release of medical information, and in-house incident reporting. Some facilities have formal written policies relating to risk management requirements and techniques. New York, among other states, has had mandatory state reporting requirements for patient-related incidents for several years. Reported incidents may be followed up by state investigations. Additional states are considering this type of system. In 1988 the Joint Commission on Accreditation of Healthcare Organizations began to require that accredited hospitals undertake risk management and that there be communication between those responsible for that function and those responsible for hospital quality assurance.

There are no similar requirements for private offices of physicians and other health care professionals. Lack of formal requirements does not suggest that risk management is inapplicable in the private office, but rather that less thought has been given to the very real risks that occur there.

DOCUMENTATION OF CARE

Nurses and physicians are constantly reminded of the importance of documentation in patient care. The medical record is one of the primary means of communication of patient data among health care providers. When it explains the patient's care accurately, factually, and without defensive overtones, it can also prevent a malpractice case. Finally, it can be the most important piece of evidence offered in defense of a professional liability lawsuit, because it is the only contemporaneous record of the event and is often written without knowledge of the patient's outcome.

Medical record entries should be accurate and timely. Since it is not possible to record every piece of information as it is received, it is acceptable to record the information within a reasonable time after the care was rendered. For example, a labor nurse is not able to record the sequence of a complicated delivery as it occurs but can record the note after the delivery has occurred and the patients, both mother and baby, are stable. Some professional judgment is necessary as a nurse decides what to note in the medical record. Vital signs, intravenous fluid and infusion rates, fetal heart rates, and contraction rates should be recorded every time they are taken, even though the values are normal. If aspects of care critical to the care of a particular patient are not recorded, a jury may be entitled to assume that the care was not rendered. Other aspects of care need not be noted where evidence can be offered of nursing routine. For example, the fact of a patient's normal skin integrity need not be noted after the admission notes in many cases. The first subsequent note about skin integrity may appear when the skin first appears impaired.

Medical record notes should consist of correct, legible information. Generally, the use of abbreviations in charting is not desirable, but it is inevitable as a time-saving device. Therefore, the staff should conform to hospital policy about accepted abbreviations and avoid obscure ones. Each medical record entry should be timed, dated, and signed. Information in the record should be objective; it should not discuss third parties unless that information is important to the care of the patient. Observations of the patient should be described in as concrete a manner as possible. For example, a reference to poor patient cooperation is not as useful as a description of those aspects of care in which the patient refused to cooperate.

Errors in a medical record should be corrected in accordance with hospital or office policy. This usually requires that errors not be erased. Instead, a line should be made through the incorrect entry and the error initialed. Occasionally, a nurse or other health care provider forgets to record information and leaves the premises. There are two possible solutions to this problem. If the information is important to the care of the patient, the nurse may call the current treating nurse and transmit the information. The receiving nurse then may write a note about the telephone call and record the information. The staff member may also record the information in the medical record the next day, but that note should not be backdated. Medical record entries should not be altered after they have been made and the record completed. It is much easier, for example, to explain why a nurse forgot to sign a note than it is to explain what else she did with the record when she signed the entry months later.

MEDICAL RECORDS

Creation of Records

Some states explicitly require that whenever a patient receives medical care a medical record must be created. Hospital accrediting organizations uniformly have similar requirements. Regardless of state or accreditation requirements, all hospitals and offices create some sort of record for each patient. A state may require that the medical record be maintained either in its original form or on microfilm for a specified period of time, but the period varies among states. In Connecticut, for example, state regulations require that a hospital maintain its record for 25 years after the discharge of the patient,[1] while many other states do not address the question of record retention. Federal regulations require, as a condition of participation in federal reimbursement programs, that hospitals retain medical records for a period "not less than that determined by the statute of limitations in" that state.[2] These state and federal requirements relate to minimum time periods; no statute or regulation requires that the records be discarded after any particular period of time.

A few states now require that licensed health care providers retain their practice medical records for a specified period of time after patients' last visits. Where states have these requirements, the retention period is usually shorter than that required of hospitals.

Hospital or office policy should define the contents of a medical record. In an office, almost everything pertaining to the patient goes into the patient's file. This is not true in a hospital. Backup laboratory records, x-rays, and other materials may be kept in separate locations throughout the hospital. Fetal monitoring tracings are often not maintained as part of the medical record, because they are bulky. Where records, such as x-rays and fetal monitoring tracings, are kept separately personnel should have prompt access to recent records, even at night or on weekends.

Written history and progress notes are almost always considered part of the patient's medical record. It is just as important to record information from telephone calls, even when they occur to another office location or to the health care provider at home. Many office practices have designed special pads on which messages are recorded at home; these forms can be placed directly into a patient's medical record on the first office day after the call.

Maintenance of Records

After defining the contents of medical records the office or facility must set retention and storage policies, particularly for those materials not covered by relevant state law. Lawsuits may be filed several years after the events in the case. This is especially true in obstetrics. Fetal monitoring tracings, for example, should be maintained for at least five years after the infant is delivered. These tracings may be moved to a safe storage facility but should remain reasonably available if needed. There is usually no reason to keep the hard copy of a fetal monitor tracing if there is a computer disk copy, although the staff may wish to preserve tracings that contain pertinent handwritten information not included on the disk copy.

Release of Records

Medical records are the property of the facility or office that created them, but many states have passed statutes requiring release of medical records under certain circumstances. Generally, a patient may request that a copy of his or her medical record be sent to a subsequent treating physician, and in some states a patient may request a copy of the medical record for personal use. The patient's legal representative may receive a copy of the record with the patient's written permission. An office or facility may charge a reasonable fee for copying and handling.

Permission from a patient to release medical information should be in writing and signed by the patient or the parent of a minor patient. There should be general policies governing release of medical information in special circumstances. For example, even if parents are divorced and one parent has custody, either parent may authorize release of the child's medical records unless a court has terminated parental rights.

Occasionally, a patient asks to read the medical record while still hospitalized. A facility may decline this request until discharge when the record has been completed. If the facility wishes to be more flexible, a patient may be allowed to see the record. Some judgment should be exercised, however, since the medical record of a psychiatric patient, for example, may contain information that may be harmful to the therapeutic environment. Where a patient is permitted to examine an original record, a staff member should be present to explain terminology and answer questions as well as to maintain the integrity of the record. Most facilities decline to copy the records of inpatients, because the record is not complete and changes in the record during hospitalization may cause questioning about the veracity of the record. Exceptions to this rule may be made where the medical record is important to a court proceeding (for example, a temporary custody hearing in a child abuse case or a probable cause hearing in a criminal matter where the victim is still in the hospital).

Tracking Clinical Information

The patient's medical record should contain all the information that is relevant to the patient's clinical care, but getting the information to the record is sometimes difficult. One of the largest areas of concern is the tracking and review of laboratory results.

Obstetrical patients undergo prenatal screening that ranges from routine blood work, such as venereal disease testing and determinations of blood type and Rh factor, to the more complex evaluation needed by women who have cervical cancer, diabetes, or lupus erythematosus. Where blood work is drawn on the premises, personnel must be sure that the specimen is labeled or tagged before it is placed with specimens from other patients. The medical record should reflect that certain testing was done so that the results can be checked at the next visit. Where the tests ordered are not routine or where an outside laboratory is used, the staff may wish to establish a log to record the tests. A log will enable the staff to note when results were received (or more to the point, not received), and when and who made any necessary contact with the patient about the results.

Laboratory results are often returned to the clinician whose name is on the requisition. The office clinician should read the results and initial the form, thus noting that the results have been seen. Clerical staff should not file laboratory results that are not initialed. Where the clinician will not be in the office for a period of time, another staff member should be designated to review incoming laboratory results.

The failure to note abnormal screening test results can compromise further testing and treatment and also result in legal problems. For example, it is difficult to defend a case where an abnormal Rh titer value is simply filed without review, and the fetus suffers compromise that might have been prevented.

POLICIES AND PROCEDURES

Health care facilities and offices often maintain policies and procedures about both personnel and patient care matters. Drafting of these documents requires considerable attention to ensure compliance with state regulatory and accrediting agency requirements. Some facilities prefer to have many policies as a way of assuring that the functions of the facility and its personnel are appropriate. Others feel that some matters are usefully addressed by policy and others are best left to professional judgment of the staff. When a decision is made to draft a policy or procedure, appropriate members of the staff should contribute to it. The language should be broad enough to accommodate permissible variations in practice but narrow enough to make the recommendations or requirements clear.

Policies can be interpreted as guidelines or requirements for the staff, depending on the language. If a member of the staff violates a policy that constitutes a requirement, that individual can be subject to discipline. In a lawsuit involving a policy violation, the facility and its staff must explain why the clinical situation made the action mandated by the policy potentially or actually more harmful than the action that was taken in that particular situation. It is preferable that the staff not be forced to violate hospital policy to provide the best patient care, so policies should be drafted with careful consideration of this possibility.

Hospital and office policies and procedures are often requested by plaintiffs during a lawsuit. The relevant policy is the one in effect at the time of the incident, not the one in effect at the time the request is made (although comparison may be interesting). Copies of old policies and procedures should be kept by each department for a reasonable number of years after they have become outdated. This requires planning since many policies are on word processors now and once changes are made in the file, there may be no hard copy to maintain. If the department cannot maintain the files, copies of outdated policies and procedures should be sent to the risk management department for storage.

Incident Reporting

The reporting of incidents that may or may not have legal implications but usually have risk management consequences is now required in many offices and in most hospitals. As noted above, some states also require licensed hospitals to report certain incidents to state authorities. The definition of a reportable incident varies with the purpose of the reporting requirement. Hospitals often define by policy the types of incidents that should be reported. These may include medication errors, patient falls, transport and communication problems among departments, and other incidents whether or not they result in patient harm. Hospitals use these data to prepare for litigation in some cases, but more commonly they use the information to identify patterns and problems within the system so that remedies can be found.

Incident reports in health care facilities should not substitute for adequate medical record documentation of patient injuries. The facility may use the same incident report form for injuries to visitors, but it often has a specially designed form for employee injuries.

Distribution of report forms within a health care facility is not standardized and may depend on how the information will be used. If the incident is serious, a staff member may not use a standard incident report. A letter to the hospital attorney that describes the problem may be more appropriate. An incident report should not be included in a patient's record nor should the clinical note in the record say that the report has been filed.

Although hospitals would prefer to keep incident reports protected and private during a later professional liability lawsuit, the court trend seems to be moving toward ordering release except where their specific use is peer review or where they are clearly prepared in anticipation of litigation. The information provided on the form, therefore, should be complete and factual but nonjudgmental. No personal comments about staff members should be made.

In addition to incident reports, some staff members keep personal notes they make about remarkable incidents that occur at work. Unless these notes are addressed to and sent to an attorney (thus protecting them under the attorney-client privilege), they may be releasable in later lawsuits if staff members are deposed. Care should be taken in drafting them.

Special Obstetrical Occurrence Reporting

Several associations and many health care facilities have designed professional liability early warning systems. These have been defined as "criterion-based techniques used by health care providers for identifying adverse patient occurrences or untoward events that may signify the emergence of potential liabilities."[3] Some of these systems are adapted from insurance company reporting criteria that have long included unanticipated serious patient outcomes, such as death, loss of body part or function, or neurological damage. Although these adverse occurrences may not be a natural result of the patient's disease or treatment, they also do not necessarily result from negligent conduct by the health care provider.

Exhibit 11–1 lists some outcome screening criteria relevant to obstetrics that can be used to design an early warning system. There are two

Exhibit 11—1   Sample Obstetrical Screening Criteria for an Early Warning System

---

Maternal or infant death.
Apgar less than 6 at one minute or less than 8 at five minutes.
Infant injury (for example, brachial palsy).
High forceps delivery.
Transfer to intensive care unit or to another hospital because of complications.
Maternal eclampsia.
Newborn resuscitation.
Prolapsed cord.
Unplanned maternal return to operating room or unplanned removal, injury, or repair
   of an organ during an operative procedure.
Maternal blood loss requiring transfusion.
Second-stage labor greater than two hours.
Failed induction.
Failed vacuum or forceps delivery.
Delivery of an infant weighing less than 2,500 g or with respiratory distress syndrome
   following a planned repeat cesarean section.
Unplanned maternal readmission.
Cord pH of less than 7.18.
Inborn term infant with seizures prior to discharge.
Pregnancy after tubal ligation.

Note: The above criteria do not include more general criteria such as medication errors and patient
falls.
See also: Obstetric clinical indicators in: American College of Obstetricians and Gynecologists,
Quality Assurance in Obstetrics and Gynecology, 1989.

---

general methods used to collect the data. The first employs focused occurrence reporting. The staff uses a set of reporting criteria to evaluate outcomes and is required to report these to a designated person (a risk manager or hospital attorney) within a specified period of time. The usual hospital incident reports are a form of focused occurrence reporting. In the second method, data are collected by using occurrence screening in record review at specified times during the hospitalization or at discharge. The reviewers use the specified outcome criteria to determine reportable incidents. When a review is completed at discharge, they have the advantage of knowing patient outcome.

The board of directors of the American Society for Hospital Risk Management of the American Hospital Association has endorsed the use of professional liability early warning systems but does not recommend a particular design. Hospitals and offices are free to design systems that will work within their practice environments.

Regardless of the type of incident reporting used, its dual purpose is to permit accumulation of data (1) to identify individual potential problems and (2) to identify patterns and trends. Where an incident reporting system identifies a pattern of patient falls, a physician whose patients experience a greater infection rate, or an increased rate of low Apgar infants, follow-up is required to collect further information. When investigation of the trend is completed, the risk management or quality assurance staff can make recommendations to address the identified problems.

Infection Control

State licensing agencies and hospital accrediting organizations require that a body within each hospital be responsible for epidemiology and infection control. In response to concerns about human immunodeficiency virus (HIV) and hepatitis, the U.S. Department of Labor and the U.S. Department of Health and Human Services in October 1987 issued a joint advisory to health care employers. The document instructed employers to categorize the tasks their employees were required to perform by likelihood of exposure to infectious materials and to ensure that those employees were adequately trained in the precautions necessary for their protection.[4] Health care employers are now required to keep materials documenting education of employees.

While hospitals may be quite aware of what is required to protect employees from risk of infection on the job, private offices have lagged behind. A hospital may be cited for violations of the federal Occupational Safety and Health Act if even a nonemployee physician endangers an employee by unsafe conduct. That physician's employer (partnership or professional corporation) also may be cited for failure to ensure that its employee (the physician) undertakes proper precautions. An employer also may be cited if OSHA discovers that office employees have not been trained in proper precautions for contact with blood and body substances or if they are not using these precautions. Fines can range as high as $10,000 per violation and are not covered by applicable insurance.

Every hospital and office practice should have policies on universal precautions and other relevant infection control practices. Repeated failure to comply must subject the employee, staff member, or physician to discipline.

IN-SERVICE EDUCATION

A health care employer has an obligation to ensure that its employees remain competent to practice. Hospitals provide in-service education as one method of keeping the staff up to date in its practice specialty. Programs should include theory and practice where appropriate. Speakers should allow adequate time for audience discussion and questions. Attendance at in-service education programs should be documented, even in those states that do not require continuing education credits for relicensure.

Patient case rounds are a common teaching tool in obstetrics, especially in services that use housestaff. Nursing staffs should be encouraged to organize their own case rounds and to attend other available clinical rounds. Opportunities to discuss clinical care retrospectively can be useful as in-service educational and communication tools.

SUMMARY

Nursing and physician staffs are now attending to risk management concerns and techniques more often even when they are not aware of it. Nurses who organize a nursing ethics discussion about how to document a difficult clinical issue are addressing ethical, legal, and risk management concerns, just as are physicians who attempt to allocate primary responsibility for delivery room newborn resuscitation. Except in very rare instances, legal and risk management concerns need not dictate answers to clinical questions. Instead, the principles and the law should be used along with clinical and practical information to guide clinical decision making. No matter what techniques are used, it is still true that provision of the best clinical care is the best risk management. Neither risk management nor the law insists that decisions made by a health care provider are required to have been correct. The decisions, however, must be shown to have been reasonable prospectively under the circumstances at the time they were made.

NOTES

1. Conn. Agencies Regs. Section 19–13–D3.
2. 42 *C.F.R.* Section 405.1026(b).
3. American Hospital Association, *Compendium of Professional Liability Early Warning Systems for Health Care Providers* (Chicago, Ill.: AHA, May 1986), 1.
4. *Federal Register* 52:41818 (October 30, 1987).

SUGGESTED READINGS

American College of Obstetricians and Gynecologists. May 1989. *Quality assurance in obstetrics and gynecology.* Washington, D.C.: ACOG.

American Hospital Association. November 1987. *AIDS and the law: Responding to the special concerns of hospitals.* Chicago, Ill.: AHA.

Burnum, J. 1989. The misinformation era: The fall of the medical record. *Annals of Internal Medicine* 110 (March 15): 482.

Gostin, L. 1989. Public health strategies for confronting AIDS: Legislative and regulatory policy in the United States. *Journal of the American Medical Association* 261:1621–630.

Kearns, K. Universal precautions: Employee resistance and strategies for planned organizational change. *Hospital & Health Services Administration* 33 (Winter): 4.

Lewis, H. 1987. Acquired immunodeficiency syndrome: State legislative activity. *Journal of the American Medical Association* 258 (November 6): 2410.

Matthews, G., and V. Neslund. 1987. The initial impact of AIDS on public health law in the United States—1986. *Journal of the American Medical Association* 257 (January 16): 344.

Roach, W., S. Chernoff, and C. Esley. 1985. *Medical records and the law.* Rockville, Md.: Aspen Publishers, Inc.

Williams, C. 1985. Guide to hospital incident reports. *HCM Review* (Winter): 19–25.

Wing, D. 1988. Hospital legal issues. In *AIDS: A health care management response,* edited by K.D. Blanchet. Rockville, Md.: Aspen Publishers, Inc., 219–48.

Zellner, K. 1988. The employer's dilemma: The AIDS crisis. *For the Defense* 30 (May): 2.

Index
of Cases

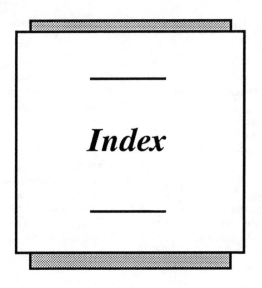

Index